Roger Williams
thinks this book
to be rather in-
adequate.

THE
THIRD FRENCH
REPUBLIC,
1870-1914

EUROPE SINCE 1500: *A Paperbound Series*

Enlightened Despotism / JOHN G. GAGLIARDO

Franco's Spain / STANLEY G PAYNE

The Third French Republic, 1870–1914 / ALEXANDER SEDGWICK

Fascist Italy / ALAN CASSELS

THE
THIRD FRENCH
REPUBLIC,
1870–1914

Alexander Sedgwick

UNIVERSITY OF VIRGINIA

THOMAS Y. CROWELL COMPANY

NEW YORK / ESTABLISHED 1834

To the memory of MARK DEWOLFE HOWE

Preface

Recent histories of the Third Republic have focused on the period between 1914 and 1940, because the events of that period appear to have great relevance to our own time. The period between 1870 and 1914 seems less dramatic, except for the Boulanger crisis and the Dreyfus affair, and it is usually treated by historians as an introduction to the critical inter-war period. Early histories of the Republic written before the fall of France in 1940 tend to emphasize the triumph of parliamentary democracy as well as the stable condition of French society and politics at the turn of the century. The conviction is strongly implied in many of these works that the Republic was synonymous with progress. A re-examination of the formative years of the Third Republic in the light of subsequent events—such as the collapse of the Third and Fourth Republics and the emergence of the formidable General De Gaulle as the dominant figure in French political life today—enables the historian to have a clear view of what France was like after almost a century of political upheaval as well as an understanding of how she was preparing herself for the dramatic challenges of the twentieth century.

An analysis of France between 1870 and 1914 reveals the conservative nature of French society and institutions. Traditional values were still very much in evidence at the end of the nineteenth century despite the great Revolution of 1789, the Revolutions of 1830 and 1848, and the abortive Revolution of 1871. These values reflected the needs and interests of a rural–agrarian society, but they were less viable in a society that was gradually becoming industrialized and urbanized. Until 1871, the Republican ideal had been a radical ideal, but the Third Republic was constructed to protect conservative interests. Throughout most of the nineteenth century, French politics was based primarily on constitutional questions: whether a constitutional monarchy along British lines was preferable to a Republic or to a Bonapartist dictatorship. As France moved into the twentieth century, politics was based to a greater extent on economic and social questions: should the state protect vested interests, or should it concern itself with the welfare of underprivileged social groups?

There are, of course, other reasons for undertaking a reexamination of French history during the early period of the Third French Republic. This was the period when France constructed a world empire second only to that of Great Britain. In the present age of colonial dissolution, a clearer understanding of the reasons for French imperialism and the contribution that French imperialism made to the national development and international stability seems imperative. The period between 1870 and 1914 was one of international tension involving "defensive alliances" and a dangerous arms race. An understanding of France's role in the chain of events leading up to World War I might contribute to a clearer understanding of similar problems in our own time. Finally, the years between 1870 and 1914 were years of great intellectual and artistic vitality. The historian must take this vitality into account in assessing the decline of the revolutionary *élan* after 1871 because intellectual and cultural developments are always intimately connected with the political side of life in France.

I would like to thank Mr. Stanley Duane, the general editor of this series, who waited patiently for a manuscript that was long overdue and Mr. Darden Asbury Pyron who helped in the preparation of the manuscript. I am profoundly grateful to Professors Nathanael Greene of Wesleyan University and Alan Ritter of the University of Virginia for their very helpful suggestions, and, finally, I am indebted to my wife, Charlene M. Sedgwick for her valuable editorial advice.

Alexander Sedgwick, Charlottesville, Virginia

Contents

1 / The Republic Takes Root, 1870–1879   1

    THE FRANCO-PRUSSIAN WAR AND THE FOUNDING OF
       THE REPUBLIC   1
    THE COMMUNE   4
    THE MONARCHIST REPUBLIC   9
    THE SEIZE MAI CRISIS   12
    THE INSTITUTIONS OF THE REPUBLIC   15

2 / The Economic and Social Condition of France,
    1870–1914   19

    POPULATION   20
    AGRICULTURE   22
    INDUSTRIAL DEVELOPMENT   25
    ECONOMIC GROWTH IN FRANCE   28
    THE ARISTOCRACY   29
    THE PEASANTS   31
    THE BOURGEOSIE   32
    THE INDUSTRIAL PROLETARIAT   34

3 / The Republic Endures, 1879–1899   39

    THE FIRST ANTICLERICAL CAMPAIGN   39
    GAMBETTA AND FERRY   44
    THE BOULANGER CRISIS   45
    THE RALLIEMENT   52
    FRENCH SOCIALISM   57
    THE PANAMA SCANDAL AND THE DREYFUS AFFAIR   61

4 / The Politics of Radicalism, 1899–1914   70

    THE SECOND ANTICLERICAL CAMPAIGN   70
    THE ACTION FRANCAISE   75
    THE LEFT   77
    THE NATIONALIST REVIVAL   84
    THE INCOME TAX AND THE ELECTION OF 1914   86

5 / France's Role in World Affairs, 1870–1914   90

    FRENCH IMPERIAL EXPANSION   90
    FRENCH DIPLOMACY   99

6 / The Revolt against Positivism   112

    THE TRIUMPH OF SCIENCE AND TECHNOLOGY   112
    ARTISTS AND INTELLECTUALS IN REVOLT   120

7 / "The Good Old Days"   130

    Bibliography   135

    Index   141

THE
THIRD FRENCH
REPUBLIC,
1870-1914

1 / The Republic
Takes Root, 1870-1879

THE FRANCO-PRUSSIAN WAR AND THE FOUNDING
OF THE REPUBLIC

The Third French Republic, like the First, was born of war.
The Prussian troops invading France in August 1870 destroyed
the Second Empire just as in August 1792 Prussian troops on
French soil contributed to the destruction of the monarchy. On
September 4, 1870, Jules Favre and Léon Gambetta, who had
been Republicans under the Second Empire, proclaimed the Republic. The "Government of National Defense" with these two as
its principal members was organized to ensure that the German
armies would be thrown back and that the regime would be
established securely. But the Prussian military leadership was a
far more competent one in 1870 than it had been in 1792; and on
September 16, the siege of Paris began.

However, the situation for France was not a hopeless one.
The Parisian garrison was reinforced by two well-trained regi-
ments that had been brought back from Rome, where they had
been protecting the Vatican. Under siege at Metz, Marshal Bazaine had command of 170,000 troops, which, if released, could
be used for a counteroffensive. When Bismarck demanded Alsace
and Lorraine, the French stiffened their will to fight, and on
October 8 Minister of the Interior Gambetta left Paris for Tours
to raise fresh troops. A new army was soon recruited; but, although the troops were fairly well clothed and armed, they

1

lacked training and experience. Leadership, particularly at the lower echelons, was inadequate because most of the regular officer corps were either in Paris or in Metz or were prisoners of war.

On October 27, the French suffered a sharp setback when Bazaine, who could have held out longer, surrendered. Before giving up the troops and the city to the Prussians, he had tried to get Bismarck to agree to the restoration of the Empire; but, failing at that, Bazaine felt that further resistance would be futile. The newly recruited army, despite some victories, was unable to raise the siege of Paris. The poorly conditioned troops became discouraged and discipline broke down; and by January, it was clear to most people that Gambetta's efforts to become another "organizer of victory" had failed. The capital city began to feel the effects of the four-month siege combined with the hardships of a particularly severe winter. The food supply was dwindling, and prices were soaring. Those who could afford the expense survived by eating the bears and elephants from the zoo, while the poor had to be content with dining on rats. When the Prussians began to bombard the city, the Republican government, which had hoped to achieve a miraculous and glorious victory, decided to accept a humiliating peace treaty.

Adolphe Thiers, former minister of King Louis Philippe (1830–1848) and historian of the Consulate and First Empire, an old man whose career supposedly was finished, was the individual chiefly responsible for restoring peace to France. He had not served in the Ministry of National Defense but had attempted on his own to get support from foreign powers by visiting London, St. Petersburg, and Vienna, but his efforts were without success. In early November, he had seen the Prussian chancellor at Versailles, hoping to work out an armistice, but negotiations failed. On the night of January 27, 1871, Jules Favre, Minister of Foreign Affairs, accepted Bismarck's terms for an armistice. The terms included the capitulation of Paris and a twenty-one day truce so that France could elect a National Assembly and establish a government with the authority to work out the conditions of peace. Gambetta, who still believed that the survival of the Republic depended upon victory, resigned his office in disgust.

The elections were held on February 8, and the results indicated that the nation as a whole, with the exception of Jacobin Paris, was weary of war and anxious to come to terms with the new German Empire. The newly elected deputies convened at Bordeaux, far from the pressures of the invading army and the Parisian mobs, and Thiers was named chief executive of the French Republic. On February 19, Thiers and Favre set out for Versailles where they were to negotiate the peace preliminaries with Bismarck. The terms laid down by the Germans included the cession of all of Alsace and part of Lorraine to the new empire, the payment of an "indemnity" by France of five billion gold francs (roughly one billion dollars), and a victory march of the German army through Paris (which did take place on March 3 with streets deserted and windows closed). These terms, which were ratified by the Treaty of Frankfurt on May 10, were exceedingly harsh. France yielded a million and a half citizens, two important cities—Strasbourg and Metz—and valuable forests and iron ore deposits as well as industrial factories. She had to pay an indemnity far in excess of the cost of the war to Germany while agreeing to the occupation of eastern France by German troops until it was paid in full. The National Assembly voted to accept the terms on March 1, and those who dissented, including Gambetta, Georges Clemenceau (the future Radical leader), and other deputies from Paris and the lost provinces, immediately resigned their seats.

The National Assembly elected in February was as much opposed to the existence of a Republican regime as it was anxious to restore peace. Of the approximately six hundred deputies who gathered at Bordeaux, well over four hundred were Monarchists of one form or another. There are a number of reasons for this. The elections were hastily contrived, half the country was occupied by enemy troops, it was difficult to set up electoral committees to nominate candidates and to organize campaigns. Some of those who were elected never knew that they were candidates. Under these conditions, the more distinguished members of a given department (France was divided into administrative units called departments) were chosen as deputies, and in many areas these *notables* were Monarchists. Followers of Napoleon III could hardly have been expected to fare well in the elections because to so many people the Empire meant war. So too did the Republic because of what appeared to be the bellicose enthusiasm of Paris, and because of the authoritarian measures of Gambetta's prefects, who, in attempting to mobilize the country, had antagonized many people. The Monarchists therefore stood to gain because of the pacifist sentiments of the overwhelming majority of voters.

Adolphe Thiers was chosen to be the chief executive because of his diplomatic abilities, because he obviously appealed to the electorate which in twenty-six departments had seen to it that he was on the list of deputies, and because he was regarded as politically neutral. An Orléanist throughout most of his career, he had recently cultivated friendships in many political circles. It was believed by the majority in the Assembly that Thiers would be the head of a provisional government which would gracefully step aside once the monarchy was restored. But although the provisional nature of the government may have been reassuring to many of the deputies in Bordeaux, it was not comforting to those who wanted to secure the Republic, such as the people of Paris.

THE COMMUNE

The atmosphere in Paris in March 1871 was very different from what it had been in the previous September when there was general enthusiasm for the restoration of the Republic, which was believed capable by its very nature of victory over the Prussians. But this enthusiasm had turned to confusion and fear as the effects of the siege began to be felt—as prices soared and rumors of treason in high places circulated through the working class districts in the northern and eastern parts of the city. The belief existed in these quarters that if Paris could only be given the same degree of self-government she had when the

First Republic was proclaimed in 1792, she again would lead the nation to victory. When the armistice had been proclaimed at the end of January 1871, many Parisians quite naturally had felt betrayed. This feeling of betrayal was reflected in the anti-peace demonstrations that broke out in February and in the resignation of some of the Parisian deputies at the time of the Assembly voting on the peace treaty terms.

Many Parisians were discouraged by the results of the national elections in February. The large Monarchist majority in the Assembly threatened the very existence of the Republic, and its conservative texture indicated that the needs of the descendants of the *sans-culottes* of the Great Revolution would be treated with the same degree of sympathy as they were in June 1848 when rural France had overwhelmed radical Paris. The choice of the former Orléanist Thiers as chief executive was not encouraging to the people of the working class districts, and they were infuriated when the government cut off the salaries of the National Guard, the sole means of support for many workers. Many merchants and shopkeepers who had gone deeply into debt were faced with bankruptcy when the government proclaimed an end to the moratorium on bills and rents that had been in existence since the war broke out. Already injured by the humiliation of Prussian troops parading in her streets, Paris was further insulted by the government's decision to establish itself at Versailles.

During March, Thiers was well aware of the widespread feelings of hostility in Paris toward the government. His authority over the entire country would be weak until he was master of the capital city. Fearing the possibility of civil war, the chief executive ordered the removal of the artillery that had been used to defend the city against the Germans. Troops were sent into Paris on March 18 to carry out these orders. In the process of dragging cannon from the heights of Montmartre, they were met by an angry mob, which after a brief tussle managed to recapture the guns, and two generals as well. The mob murdered the generals while the troops—cold, hungry, and unsympathetic—fraternized with the murderers. Thiers decided to withdraw the rest of the troops from the city until the proper moment came to subdue it. Once again France was at war with her capital city.

The term "Commune" refers to the municipal institutions that governed Paris in the middle ages, and the Commune itself first became significant in French history in 1356 when Parisians turned against Charles V during the Hundred Years' War. During the French Revolution, the revived Paris Commune often quarreled with the national government. So it was quite natural in the spring of 1871, when Paris found herself at odds again with France, that she reverted to the communal form of government. On March 26 the populace (consisting mostly of workers, artisans, and petty bourgeois, since many members of the upper classes had fled the city) were called upon to elect representatives to the Commune. Of the eighty-six men elected, well over half were Republicans whose primary interest was in turning the clock back to the days of Robespierre. Twenty-six of them were workers whose ideological allegiance was divided between the Socialist theories of Marx and Proudhon. The defense of Paris was entrusted to the Central Committee of the National Guard, which commanded between 70,000 and 90,000 men in March. However, because of poor morale and lack of discipline, the number of men serving in the National Guard dropped sharply to between 30,000 and 40,000 in April.

Thiers made his move on April 2. By this time the Versailles government had roughly 130,000 men at its disposal, many of whom had only recently been released from German prison camps. Government troops seized the suburb of Courbevoie, thus beginning the second siege of Paris within six months. On the following day a National Guard unit attempted a counter-offensive, but its results were disastrous. Its leaders were summarily executed. The Commune retaliated by arresting the Archbishop of Paris and a number of priests, an act designed to satisfy anticlerical sentiments rampant in Paris and to infuriate the Catholic majority in Versailles. By the end of April, the Commune's cause was hopeless. Efforts to get help from the other communes that had sprung up in Lyons, Marseilles, St.-Etiènne, and Toulouse were futile. Moderate Paris Republican elements, who had endorsed the Commune in March, were now war-weary and disillusioned, so they abandoned the cause. During May, the Versailles army succeeded in capturing a number of outlying fortresses vital to the city's defense. On Sunday, May 16, soldiers entered the city through a gate that had been opened by a sympathizer.

Because his generals had overestimated the defense capabilities of the National Guard, Thiers became cautious and delayed his final offensive against the Commune until May 22. Once again the barricades went up in the eastern sections of the city as the communards prepared to resist the onslaught of Thiers' troops. There was a great deal of bloodshed, because many of Thiers' troops were country boys with absolutely no sympathy for Paris, and because they wanted to make up for the humiliating defeat they had suffered at the hands of the Prussians. The bloodshed was increased by the chief executive, who, eager to purge Paris of its militant elements and to establish his authority once and for all, encouraged his troops to shoot prisoners. The communards responded by executing their prisoners, including the Archbishop of Paris. The last battle was fought in the cemetery of Père Lachaise, where two hundred National Guardsmen died with their backs to a wall. The army of Versailles lost around 1000 men in the battle, while the commune lost 20,000 men, women, and children. Forty thousand communards were arrested and tried, and of the 13,000 who were sent to prison colonies in the Pacific and off the coast of South America, 3000 died as a result of the treatment they received in transit.

Marxists have seen in the struggle of the Paris Commune one of the first battles between the proletariat and the bourgeoisie. The Commune has become a heroic symbol to the Communist world—a brave effort doomed to failure because the hour of the great proletarian revolution had not yet arrived. This abortive revolution has been praised by Marx and honored by Lenin; and today, Mao Tse-tung cites the Commune as an inspirational example in his efforts to carry out a cultural revolution in China. To what extent are the Marxists correct in their assessment of the events in France in the spring of 1871? Certainly the most enthusiastic supporters of the Commune were the workers and artisans seeking legislation to maintain a high employment rate and a decent standard of living. Thiers' government feared the specter of socialism in the same way that the government of the Second Republic had feared the threat to private property in June 1848. In both 1848 and 1871, the bourgeois instinct to defend property rights overcame the bourgeois belief in social justice, which accounts in large part for the bloodbaths that occurred in Paris on both occasions. The fact that many of those who were deported and exiled were Socialists indicates that the government in Versailles came to much the same conclusions about the Commune as did Marx.

To what extent did the Commune try to implement socialist principles? If public ownership of the means of production is regarded as a fundamental socialist principle, then the Commune was scarcely inclined in that direction. It did seize some abandoned shops with the idea of turning them into public workshops; it did think of setting up credit facilities at the expense of the pawnshops; but its respect for private property was such that it did not repudiate debts or confiscate the resources of the Bank of France, choosing instead to borrow money. The program supported by the Commune—separation of Church and State, compulsory education, freedom of association, and freedom of the press—was, for the most part, to be enacted by governments of the Third Republic by 1914. Its most radical social legislation was to prohibit night work in the bakeries.

If class conflict contributed to the outbreak of civil war in 1871, it cannot be regarded as the sole cause. The old Jacobin spirit, frustrated by a humiliating defeat, was also responsible. Perhaps as important as anything else in the causal pattern of the civil war was the old conflict between rural and urban France, a conflict which had contributed to the outbreak of the Revolution in 1789. Paris, Marseilles, Lyons and other cities that were feeling the effects of industrialization and the pressure of population increases attempted to set up semi-autonomous governments because they felt that a National Assembly dominated by rural interests would not pay sufficient attention to the problems of urbanization, nor would it be particularly interested in the needs of the city dweller.

Nationally, the effects of the defeat of the Paris Commune were considerable. Political divisions and social tensions that had existed since 1789 became accentuated, and it was to be a long time before the bitterness on both sides would subside. The socialist movement received a serious setback adversely affecting the political Left as a whole, although this was not immediately apparent. Ironically, the Versailles government's victory over the Commune strengthened rather than weakened the Republican regime. Before the events of the spring of 1871, to a great many Frenchmen, the Republic had meant war and disorder; but now that the Parisian Jacobins had been crushed, they felt that the Republic might be capable of maintaining peace and restoring order and was worthy of support.

THE MONARCHIST REPUBLIC

The fact that the Republic was becoming more popular throughout the country was made clear in the by-elections held in July 1871, in which Republicans won an overwhelming majority of seats, a trend that continued in the local elections of 1871 and 1872. At the same time, the prestige of Adolphe Thiers, the man most responsible for this turn of events, reached a new high. Between 1871 and 1873, a period sometimes known as the reign of Adolphe I, Thiers came to the conclusion that the Republic was capable of providing conservative government and that it was the form of government that divided Frenchmen the least. Instead of serving the interests of the Monarchists, in whose ranks he had until recently belonged, the former historian of the Napoleonic era began to favor a Republic with a strong executive similar to that of the Consulate. In 1873, when the indemnity was paid off—eighteen months ahead of schedule— and the last Prussian soldier had quitted French soil, Thiers seemed to be both indispensable and indestructible.

The Monarchists were becoming alarmed not only because

of mounting Republican strength, but because of their own weaknesses. French Monarchists fell into two groups: those who followed the Comte de Chambord, grandson of the last Bourbon king, Charles X (1824–30), and those who followed the Comte de Paris, grandson of Louis Philippe. The Comte de Chambord's supporters, often called legitimists or *ultras,* were not particularly enthusiastic about cooperating with the Comte de Paris and his supporters, the Orléanists. They had not forgotten the Revolution of 1830 that had caused Charles X to be removed from the throne of his ancestors to be replaced by his cousin Louis Philippe. The legitimists were further galled by the fact that the Comte de Paris' great-grandfather, the Duc d'Orléans (Philippe Égalité), as a member of the revolutionary Convention, had voted for the execution of Louis XVI.

The major difference between the *ultra* mentality and the Orléanist mentality lay in their respective attitudes toward the French Revolution. Most legitimists simply wanted to revive as much as possible of the Old Regime. The Orléanists were essentially parliamentarians, and they favored the sort of constitutional monarchy that had been established during the first phase of the Revolution (1789–92), and re-established under Louis Philippe. Monarchists of both groups, however, felt that the Comte de Chambord should come to the throne and, since he had no children, proclaim the Comte de Paris as his heir. Orléanists and some legitimists became very upset when, in July 1871, Chambord returned to France after a lifetime in exile and issued a manifesto that in effect declared he would accept the throne only if he could reign according to the principles established by his grandfather. This refusal to compromise with the demands of post-revolutionary France further weakened the Monarchist cause at the time when the Republic was gaining strength from the by-elections. As Thiers' position became stronger and he became less interested in a restoration, Monarchists became convinced that the former Orléanist would have to go. After much parliamentary maneuvering, a resolution designed to embarrass Thiers was passed in the Assembly on May 24, 1873; and the chief executive, recognizing that he no longer had the support of a parliamentary majority even though he had considerable popular support, was forced to resign. Marshal MacMahon, a Monarchist, was elected President of the Republic. The real issue involved in the crisis of May 24 was whether the Republic should be continued on a provisional basis or should be established as a permanent regime. If it should be the latter, the National Assembly would have to provide it with permanent institutions.

After the Monarchists, headed by MacMahon's chief minister, the Duc de Broglie, had succeeded in obtaining Thiers' downfall, they decided to approach the Comte de Chambord again to see if he might have tempered his goals to a more realistic position. The Comte de Paris visited the pretender in his residence in the mountains of Austria. The cordiality of the meeting encouraged Monarchists to believe that Chambord was willing to compromise. But their hopes were shattered on October 27, 1873, when a Bonapartist newspaper published a letter the pretender had written to one of his followers declaring that as king he would never accept the tricolored flag, that he would have to take as the national standard the white flag of the Bourbons. Everyone except his most ardent supporters realized then that Henry V of France would never achieve the throne.

The only course left for the Monarchist majority in the National Assembly was to stall for time. The legitimists would never allow the Comte de Paris to become king as long as his cousin lived. On November 23, 1873, the Law of the Septennate was passed. This made MacMahon's term of office seven years, during which time the Monarchist majority fervently hoped a miracle might occur to bring the restoration to pass.

A growing number of deputies in Versailles were becoming aware of the stubborn facts of political life. There was pressure from the country to dissolve the Assembly and to hold new elections; but this would mean that radical Republicanism might make impressive gains because of the political organizations that were being set up all over France by Léon Gambetta and his followers. Bonapartists were making impressive gains in local and by-elections, and this offended the sensibilities of most deputies who were devoted to the parliamentary tradition that Bonapartism repudiated. Napoleon III had died in England in 1873, but his son, the Prince Imperial, was about to come of age, and there was every reason to believe that he would have a certain charismatic appeal. The question that posed itself in the minds of French politicians in 1875 was whether to establish a Republican regime that would be acceptable to some Monarchists or to run the risks of either Radical victories at the polls or another Bonapartist *coup d'état*. They chose the first.

On January 30, 1875, a constitutional law was passed regulating the election of the President of the Republic. By the end of the following month a number of constitutional laws were enacted that would provide the Third Republic with permanent institutions, including a bicameral legislature. What had caused a Monarchist Assembly to establish Republican institutions? The first constitutional law, to be sure, had been passed by one vote, but those who voted for it included Orléanists whose interest in parliamentary supremacy was much greater than their interest in a king, conservative Republicans like Thiers, and finally Gambetta and some of his supporters who believed that a conservative Republic was better than no Republic at all. Gambetta had originally argued that the Assembly did not have constituent powers and that another election was required before a constituent assembly could come into being. His willingness to compromise instead of holding out for a more radical solution to the constitutional problems was a major factor in establishing the Third Republic. On December 31, 1875, the National Assembly, which had been elected in 1871 to restore peace to the country, adjourned to make way for the new constitutional system.

THE *SEIZE MAI* CRISIS

In 1876, the Republic existed in theory more than in actual fact. The President of the Republic, Marshal MacMahon, was a Monarchist. The newly elected Senate, because of the electoral procedure established in 1875, which favored the more conservative elements in the country, was also Monarchist. Only the Chamber of Deputies, the lower house, had a Republican majority. The elections of 1876—despite all the pressure that the President and other conservative leaders brought to bear on prefects (the chief administrative officials in the departments), schoolteachers, and clergy to secure a Monarchist victory— produced a Chamber composed of 340 genuine Republicans, 30 timid Republicans, 75 Monarchists, and 75 Bonapartists. Issues such as French aid to Pope Pius IX in his struggle against the new Kingdom of Italy and the role of the Catholic Church in education were difficult to resolve; and, given the fundamental disagreement between Monarchists and Republicans on these issues, friction was inevitable. Ministers found it difficult to adopt a policy that would suit the two chambers and the President. MacMahon was becoming alarmed by the anticlerical sentiments of the Chamber of Deputies, sentiments that threatened to undermine the judiciary, the civil service, and the officer corps as well as the educational system, all of which were bastions of conservatism. The Duc de Broglie and Mgr. Dupanloup, Bishop of Orléans, along with other Monarchist leaders, succeeded in persuading the Marshal that a showdown with the Chamber was unavoidable. If the President of the Republic, with the consent of the Senate, dissolved the Chamber (which he was legally entitled to do), then the electorate would have the opportunity to decide between the conservative policies of MacMahon and De Broglie and the more radical policies of the lower house.

On May 16 (*seize mai*), 1877, MacMahon forced Prime Minister Jules Simon, a moderate Republican, to resign. The extent to which the ministers were responsible to the President or to the Chamber had not been clearly established by the constitutional laws of 1875. MacMahon thought that he was perfectly within his rights to replace Simon with De Broglie, who was more sympathetic to his views. The Republican majority in the Chamber disagreed, contending that the ministers were primarily responsible to the legislature and that the President of the Republic was merely a figurehead. The Chamber refused to endorse the new ministry, a deadlock ensued, and MacMahon with the consent of the Senate dissolved the Chamber of Deputies and called for new elections. Once again the Monarchists brought every pressure to bear on the electorate to affect the outcome. To gain sympathy, the Republicans used the occasion of Thiers' death to stage an elaborate funeral for the man who had done so much to help their cause and who had been so badly treated by the Monarchists. On October 14, 1877, the voters returned 320 Republicans and 200 Conservatives (Monarchists and Bonapartists included).

Two fundamental issues were resolved by the constitutional crisis of *seize mai:* first, Republican policies were approved by 54 percent of the electorate, which meant that the Republic was the preferred form of government; second, ministers were to be responsible to the legislature, and the power of the President of the Republic was to be curtailed drastically. MacMahon bowed to the will of the voters by appointing a Republican ministry; but, although the chief of state would continue to have the legal authority to dissolve the Chamber with the consent of the Senate, never again in the life of the Third Republic was the authority used.

Republicans took complete control of the Republic in 1879. MacMahon remained in office throughout 1878 in order to preside over the International Exposition, which took place as a demonstration to the world that France had recovered from the humiliation of 1870. The Senatorial elections of January 1879 produced a Republican majority in the upper house. President MacMahon was angered by Republican insistence that Monarchists be purged from the upper ranks of the army and magistracy. Finally, on January 30, realizing that the Monarchist cause was hopeless, he resigned. He was replaced almost immediately by a Republican of long standing, Jules Grévy, who announced that he would never oppose the general will of the nation as it was embodied in the legislature. By the end of the year the government had returned to Paris, the *Marseillaise* was officially recognized as the national anthem, and the motto of the Republic, "Liberty, Equality, Fraternity," was engraved on all the public buildings. But high above Paris on Montmartre stood the gleaming white Church of Sacré-Coeur, built under the auspices of the Monarchist Assembly to atone for the sins committed by revolutionary France. It was a reminder that a significant minority of Frenchmen were not Republicans and that the Republic had yet to accomplish what no regime since 1789 had been able to achieve—political union of the whole nation.

THE INSTITUTIONS OF THE REPUBLIC

The institutions adopted by the Third Republic during the decade of the 1870s reflect the political and social tensions that had plagued the country since 1789 and the problems involved in reconciling executive and legislative authority. Part of the cause of the Revolution of 1789 was the concentration of too much power in the hands of the monarch. Although the Revolution had brought into being a legislative body—the Convention—with supreme authority, the inability of this legislature to govern effectively in times of crisis resulted first in the dictatorship of the Committee of Public Safety and finally in the Napoleonic dictatorship. A proper balance between the two branches of government was not achieved during the Restoration, under the July Monarchy, under the Second Republic, or under the Second Empire. Nor was it to be achieved under the Third Republic.

The President of the Republic was elected by an absolute majority of the Senate and the Chamber of Deputies meeting together as a National Assembly. He was elected to a seven year term and was eligible for reelection. The National Assembly of 1875 wanted to avoid the mistake made in 1848 when the constitution of the Second Republic required both President and Assembly to be elected by universal manhood suffrage. In cases of conflict, both could appeal to the electorate, which is precisely what happened when Louis Napoleon as President of the Republic executed the *coup d'état* of 1851. Under the Third Republic, the chief of state owed his election to the Assembly and was therefore dependent on it. In order to assure its ascendancy, the legislature rarely elected a national figure who might overshadow it. In the shadow of war, the election of Raymond Poincaré to the presidency in 1912 proved to be the only exception to the succession of mediocrities summoned to this high office. The President of the Republic had charge of appointments to the armed forces and the civil service; he had the power to negotiate and ratify treaties, and he presided over national ceremonies. But everything of consequence that he signed had to be countersigned by a minister who was responsible to the two chambers. The real power given to the chief of state in 1875 was the right to dissolve the Chamber with the consent of the Senate, but the crisis of *seize mai* and the subsequent triumph of Republicans in the Chamber and in the Senate made use of the right of dissolution seem un-Republican because it was associated in the public mind with the Monarchist Mac-Mahon.

The Senate was intended to be a bastion of conservatism to eliminate the possibilities of a unicameral legislature encouraging radical and tyrannous policies, as it had in 1793. Seventy-five of its three hundred members were to be chosen by the outgoing Monarchist legislature in 1875. The rest were to be chosen by electoral colleges convened in the departments, which were dominated in the 1870s by monarchist and Bonapartist *notables*. The minimum age for a senatorial candidate was forty, because of the belief that age, wisdom, and conservatism were one and the same thing. A third of the Senate was elected every three years. Even though, by 1881, the electoral colleges came to be dominated by Republicans, the conservative nature of the Senate was maintained because of the predominance of rural interests. The upper house shared legislative power with the Chamber and acted as a restraining influence on radical legislation. In 1896, the lower house approved the income tax, which was then rejected by the Senate.

The Chamber of Deputies was elected every four years by universal manhood suffrage. The minimum age for a candidate was twenty-one. Because it was the national institution closest to the people, the method of electing deputies became a significant political issue. In 1871, deputies were elected by department or *scrutin de liste*. This system, which was used in 1885, in 1889, and in 1919, required that a political group or party draw up a list of candidates for each department. The voter then chose one from among a number of lists. Those who argued in favor of *scrutin de liste* pointed out that candidates were relatively free from administrative and local pressures during a campaign, and that deputies were relatively free of constituent control. The system presupposed a certain amount of party discipline, which was lacking under the Third Republic. The method for electing deputies that seemed most acceptable to Republican politicians was the *scrutin d'arrondissement* or the *scrutin uninomal*, which was defined by the Organic Law of November 30, 1875. A department was divided up into *arrondissements* or districts, each of which voted for a deputy for each 100,000 inhabitants. The candidate receiving a clear majority of the registered votes was elected deputy. If no candidate received a clear majority, a second election (*deuxième tour*) took place a week later between the candidate who had received the most votes on the first ballot and other candidates chosen—after a good deal of manipulating and maneuvering—from among the also-rans of the week before. This system made candidates and deputies much more susceptible to local pressures; until 1877, it favored monarchists; afterwards, it favored Republicans.

The Third Republic was dominated by the Chamber of Deputies. The ministers, charged with making policy decisions, were responsible to it, and ministerial stability depended upon the ability of a given ministry to maintain a parliamentary majority. In England, such a majority was maintained by a fairly disciplined two-party system. In France, there were many political parties representing different social groups and various interests. Majorities in the Chamber depended upon delicate compromises that discouraged ministries from initiating bold new policies. Ministers were often embarrassed by the *interpellation*, whereby any deputy, during the course of a debate, could demand an explanation of a given policy and call for a vote of confidence on the spot if the minister's reply failed to satisfy him. The *interpellation* made it difficult for ministers to defend a policy or to adopt a program that might be controversial. The effect of the *interpellation* on French politics was somewhat similar to the effect of the anarchical *liberum veto* on Polish politics in the eighteenth century. The *scrutin d'arrondissement* together with the *interpellation* enabled local interests to take precedence over the national interest, which, in a political system dominated by the legislature, made it hard for any government to formulate effective policy.

A weak executive and a dominant legislature—itself hampered by internal dissension—satisfied the nineteenth century Liberal tradition that favored a strong parliament and limited government. In this sense, the National Assembly was intended to act as a check on governmental action rather than as a means of implementing such action. The Orléanists and conservative Republicans who were chiefly responsible for the constitutional laws of 1875 accepted the Liberal tenet that the best government was that which governed least. Furthermore, the institutions of the Third Republic were ideally suited to an essentially conservative society that feared a strong government capable of transforming the social structure.

2 / The Economic and Social Condition of France, 1870–1914

The Third Republic came into being at a time when all of Europe was undergoing change caused by the accelerated pace of the Industrial Revolution. Industry was becoming mechanized at all levels; the family firm was being replaced by the corporation backed by innumerable stockholders capable of supplying ever greater amounts of capital. Having linked the major cities of Europe, the railroads were now moving into the isolated rural areas. New markets were being opened up all over the world. These changes affected not only Europe's economic conditions, but her social and cultural life as well. After 1870, industry superseded agriculture as the European continent's economic base. An increasing number of people were abandoning their farms and their rural heritage for the opportunities provided by the cities. The bourgeoisie dominated all phases of European life, while the importance of the aristocracy continued to decline. The workers were becoming politically self-conscious and the peasants were becoming aware of a world beyond the village limits. The political instincts of the lower classes, developed by rapid social and economic change as well as by a growing respect for education, assured the triumph of democracy in western Europe.

France was regarded by many as being the world's wealthiest nation even as late as the Second Empire (1852–70). In 1869, she had the largest population in the West except for Russia and the United States. She had the greatest agricultural resources in an age still dominated by agrarian interests. In 1860, France was second only to England in industrial production. Yet by 1914, her role in the economic life of Europe and of the world had substantially diminished despite the fact that she had acquired the world's second largest empire, an empire that made more resources and markets available to her.

POPULATION

One of the striking features of nineteenth-century French history is the relatively slow demographic growth as compared with other nations. In 1871, the new German Empire held a population of 41,000,000 as compared to France's population of 36,103,000. By 1901, the German population had reached 56 millions whereas the French had not reached 39 millions. In 1911, Great Britain had surpassed France; and in 1914, French population ranked sixth behind the United States, Russia, Germany, Austria-Hungary, and Great Britain. Between 1820 and 1901, the population of the United Kingdom including Ireland had increased by 72.5 percent despite famine and emigration. German population had increased by roughly the same amount during the same period, while French population had increased by only 19 percent. The loss of 1.5 million citizens from the annexation of Alsace and Lorraine by Germany was almost offset by Italian, Spanish, and Belgian immigrants who came to France to farm marginal lands and to take advantage of the low rents.

Demographers have attributed the slow rate of growth in France to a gradual decline in the birth rate. The decline in fertility was caused by the use of contraceptives and by abortions. Explanations as to why Frenchmen wished to limit the size of the family vary. The nineteenth-century Catholic economist Le Play argues that, because the inheritance laws embodied in the Napoleonic Code required property to be divided among children, this automatically limited the size of the family in rural areas where farms were already quite small. Others argue that there were ways to circumvent the inheritance laws without significantly affecting the size of the family. An interesting and more plausible explanation, if difficult to prove, was put forth by Paul Leroy-Beaulieu who stated that the decline in the birth rate was due to "civilization." As the bourgeoisie increased, as people became educated and more aware of creature comforts, as the possibilities for social advancement at all levels improved, many Frenchmen concluded that, by limiting the size of the family, more people would be able to share the blessings of civilization.

In 1856, 75.6 percent of the French population lived in the country; in 1886, the rural population was 64.1 percent; and by 1906, it had fallen to 57.9 percent of the total. This figure includes those not directly connected with the soil, such as village shopkeepers, schoolteachers, and administrative officials. Reasons for rural depopulation in a country that for centuries derived its strength and ideals from the soil include the abandoning of marginal lands in the face of competition from larger farms, agricultural crises that forced the self-sufficient peasants to limit the number of mouths to feed and the others to quit the farm entirely, and finally the job opportunities available to the peasants in the factory towns and in the cities.

Urban development in France at the end of the nineteenth century was less rapid and less extensive than it was in Great Britain or Germany, despite the fact that the percentage of the urban population was increasing. In 1896, there were thirty-six cities in the United Kingdom including Ireland with a population of over 100,000; there were twenty-eight in Germany in the same category and only twelve in France. Paris was by far the largest city with 2,536,834 inhabitants, followed by Lyons with 466,028, Marseilles with 442,239, Bordeaux with 256,906, Lille with 216,276, and Toulouse with 149,963 inhabitants. The gradual rather than rapid increase in the size of the French urban population as compared with England and Germany was due to the lack of severe demographic pressures and to the relatively stable land tenure system.

The slow demographic rate of growth of France had two important consequences. First, the decline in the birth rate meant that the younger generation was relatively small. In 1866, there were 4.4 million Frenchmen between the ages of twenty and thirty-four, and in 1911 there were 4.5 million in the same age group. In Germany there were 4.7 million men between the ages of twenty and thirty-four in 1871, and in 1910 there were 7.7 million men in the same category. Thus Germany was at a distinct advantage in terms of manpower available for military service. The second consequence of the slow rate of growth was its detrimental effect on economic expansion. A rapidly growing population provides a challenge for farmers and industrialists to produce more, assuming that the resources are available. This was true of England in the eighteenth century. Some economic historians have argued that this high percentage of Frenchmen in the middle and older age groups, with the greatest ability to save money but not risk their capital, discouraged economic expansion.

AGRICULTURE

The condition of French agriculture in 1870 was not very different from its condition under the Old Regime. In eighteenth century France, the land tenure system had favored the small- and medium-sized farm instead of the large estate, which it had favored in England and in eastern and southern Europe. The Revolution, which gave the peasant farmer even greater control of the land, perpetuated the land tenure system already in existence. Church lands were divided up, and the inheritance laws established under Napoleon created a veritable "land-chopping machine" by forcing the farmer to divide his small holding equally among his sons. In the 1880s, the number of French farms reached a peak of 3.5 million.

It is true that there were large estates in the region around Paris, in Normandy, in Berry, and in the Sologne in central France. The fertile soil and the example of English and Belgian agricultural techniques that increased production encouraged agriculture on a large scale. The existence of major urban centers —such as the capital and the Lille-Tourcoing-Roubaix complex in the north—stimulated agricultural development in the surrounding countryside because of increasing consumer demands on production. These regions produce wheat, beet sugar, dairy products, and wool for local, national, and foreign consumption. But the rest of France, the East, West, and the Midi, was dominated by small-ownership. The most important produce from these regions included wine, olive oil and fruit; and, although wine was produced for the world market, the tendency of the small farmer was to produce enough for himself and his family. In short, the stagnant condition of French agriculture in the nineteenth century was largely due to its being geared to a subsistence rather than a market economy. The lack of rapidly growing urban centers other than Paris, Lille, and Lyons, the poor means of transportation and communication, inadequate farm equipment, and the belief on the part of Conservatives and Republicans alike that the nation's future depended upon the self-reliant and self-sufficient peasant proprietor combined to discourage an agricultural revolution of the sort that had taken place in England and in the Low Countries.

The Third Republic was founded at a time when significant developments that would be affecting French agriculture were about to take place. In 1875, France produced a bumper wine harvest of 83 million hectoliters, a record never since equaled. Even at that time, however, the phylloxera epidemic was beginning to infect the vineyards in the Midi; and within four years it had destroyed almost half the vineyards of France. The cost of the damage done by the disease was even greater than the Prussian war debt. The vineyards were eventually saved by grafting disease-resistant vine roots brought over from the United States onto French vines, and the vineyards of the Midi were transferred from the rocky hillsides to the more fertile bottom lands. Wine production revived rapidly because of these measures and because of the Méline tariff of 1892, which restricted imports from Spain and Italy. Whereas before the phylloxera epidemic the wine producers had emphasized quality, they now emphasized quantity in hopes of making up for previous losses and avoiding competition from Algeria, which was not affected by the tariff.

Winegrowers between 1900 and 1907 found themselves with a new crisis on their hands caused by overproduction. Wine prices dropped sharply, to the detriment of the farmers in the Midi. As a result of the emphasis on wine production after the epidemic, farmers had given up raising other crops and had become entirely dependent on their vineyards. In 1907, the dreadful plight of the winegrowers resulted in riots in the South; and a messianic agitator named Marcellin Albert appeared, attempting to put pressure on the government by calling for a taxpayers' strike and the resignation of all local officials. Rebellious developments in the Midi reached such proportions that Prime Minister Clemenceau was forced to send troops into Narbonne and Montpellier where, after bloody clashes with the peasants, they finally restored order.

These crises caused wine producers not only to seek help from the government but also to help themselves by setting up organizations to protect the industry. In 1907, the *Confédération Générale des Vignérons du Midi* was formed to prevent fraud. In 1913, various regional organizations came together to form the *Fédération des Associations Viticoles*. These federations enabled wine producers to learn more about the problems of production and of the market that helped them and the economy as a whole.

Another crisis that aggravated French agriculture from 1880 to the turn of the century was caused by foreign competition. Competition from Latin America and Australia was forcing wool producers out of business. Dairy produce from Denmark and the Netherlands, wine from Spain and Italy, and wheat from the United States and Russia competed successfully in markets that had hitherto been dominated by French products. Between 1880 and 1900, land values fell and the price of grain in France dropped by a third. Those who had been eking out a marginal subsistence from the soil were forced to abandon their small farms. The crisis was rendered worse by the phylloxera epidemic and by the general economic recession which affected Europe as a whole. It resulted in 1892 in the passage by the National Assembly of the Méline Tariff, which was designed to protect agriculture and industry. This tariff, which shocked free-trade sentiment, succeeded in raising agricultural prices in France and contributed to revitalizing agriculture.

The economic depression at the end of the century was a major factor in introducing the changes that presaged what one historian has called the "agricultural revolution of the twentieth century." It stopped the increase in the number of farms by forcing peasants off the land, it helped increase production by encouraging a trend toward medium-sized farms, and it caused farmers to think more in terms of a market economy. The crisis also caused the government to take a greater interest in agricultural problems. In 1881, the Ministry of Agriculture was established, and the government began to provide technological information for farmers and encouraged farmers' cooperatives and mutual aid societies. Improved transportation and communication facilities broke down provincial barriers and helped to end the long period of agricultural stagnation.

INDUSTRIAL DEVELOPMENT

Historians considering the industrial development of France at the end of the nineteenth century and comparing it with industrial development elsewhere often stress the backward condition of the French economy as a whole. They overlook the fact that there was industrial development and economic growth even though it was less dynamic than in the United States, Great Britain, and Germany. Napoleon III had been particularly interested in industry. Railroad construction, vital to industry both in terms of materials used and in terms of the movement of goods and services, is a noted feature of the Second Empire. In 1870, France had 16,000 kilometers of railroad in operation, of which 13,000 had been added since 1851. Under the Empire, banks were encouraged to provide industry with the necessary capital to expand. The net result of these efforts was a period of slow, steady economic growth beginning in 1860 and lasting until 1882—despite the Franco-Prussian War and the loss of Alsace-Lorraine, which deprived France of a valuable industrial area. Between 1882 and 1896, industrial expansion was slowed by the agricultural crisis and its effect on consumer power, by the financial crisis of 1882, and by the depressed condition of the world economy during that period. Slow, steady economic growth began again in 1897 and lasted until the outbreak of World War I.

Governments of the Third Republic were keenly interested in industrial development. Not only did they encourage railroad construction through private enterprise, but they also provided public funds when private resources were lacking. In 1910, the French government had invested 5,700,830,000 francs in railroads, while private companies had invested 16,307,867,057 francs. The government also subsidized shipping and provided funds for canal and road construction. Government concern for industrial development at the end of the nineteenth century is reflected in the return to protectionism and in the exploitation of the French Empire.

French banking continued to play an important role in the French economy after the establishment of the Republic. The great corporate banks—the *Crédit Lyonnais,* the *Société Générale,* the *Comptoir d'Escompte*—grew rapidly; and they, together with the *Banque de Paris et des Pays-Bas* founded in 1872, provided capital for French railroads and public utilities. The success of existing banks encouraged the establishment of a number of other corporate investment banks in the 1870s, chief among which was the *Union Générale.* Eugène Bontoux, its director, attracted Catholic depositors who in an age of antisemitism did not want to patronize Jewish and Protestant firms. In 1882, the *Union Générale* crashed, setting off a major financial crisis in France. Many Catholics were convinced that the crash was caused by Jewish intrigue, and they became more hostile than ever toward the regime.

French coal mining developed rapidly after the discovery in 1847 of coalfields in northern France. Other important coal mines were located in the Loire basin and in the Midi. Between 1870 and 1914, French coal production increased steadily. The mines yielded 16,000,000 metric tons in 1872; 21,000,000 tons in 1882; 33,000,000 tons in 1900, and 41,000,000 tons in 1913. However, Great Britain in 1913 produced 292,000,000 tons of coal, and Germany produced 279,000,000 tons. French coal production was insufficient to satisfy the demands of her industry, and the country was obliged to import coal.

The availability of coal at low cost was a major factor in the industrial development of Europe in the nineteenth century. For many reasons, the cost of French coal was high: the mines were hard to work, making the pithead price high, the coalfields were far from the industrial areas, transportation facilities were poor.

The French iron and steel industry expanded steadily as a result of the impetus received from railroad construction, from shipbuilding, and from new inventions that increased production. Important iron ore deposits were located in the center of the country, in northern France, and in Lorraine, but much of that area was annexed by Germany in 1871. The loss of these iron ore deposits hampered steel production, as Bismarck had intended that it should. The iron and steel industries became stagnated between 1871 and 1890; but, in the following decade, a new furnace invented by Martin, along with other production improvements, caused a rapid increase in the output of iron and steel. In 1892, France produced 2,000,000 tons of metal; in 1908, she produced 2,400,000 tons; and in 1912, 3,775,000 tons. As a result of the new inventions, French steel output at the beginning of the twentieth century increased at a greater rate than any other country. The iron ore deposits in French Lorraine near Brieux that had been regarded as unusable until the new smelting process was discovered, served not only French industry but German and Belgian needs as well. France, which had been cut off from major deposits in 1871, found herself the world's largest exporter of iron ore in 1914.

The French textile industry also had been adversely affected by the Treaty of Frankfurt because much of it was located in Alsace. Mulhouse, a major textile center, was now a German city, but many Alsatian textile manufacturers refused to become German subjects, choosing instead to establish new factories in the Champagne region. New textile centers also emerged in the North. Handlooms were rapidly replaced by machine looms after 1871, and producers were able to find markets for the increased amount of cotton and woolen goods because of the tariff barriers and because of the French colonies, where the demand for cotton goods was especially great. The silk industry, always important to the economy as a whole, was forced to mechanize to overcome the stiff competition from Germany and Switzerland, where artificial silk was being manufactured. The protected home market together with England's free trade policy, which caused her to import more silk than France retained, caused the industry to prosper.

France has always depended heavily upon the production of luxury goods, and she continued to do so in the period between 1870 and 1914. French dresses, furniture, and cosmetics were very much in demand throughout the world. These commodities were manufactured in small shops, some of which could trace their origins back to the guilds of the Old Regime, and they helped to sustain the artisan in an age when his existence elsewhere was increasingly threatened by mechanization. France was also becoming a leading producer of another important luxury item—the automobile. The public works programs sponsored by the government had greatly improved the condition of French roads, thereby making the motor car more useful.

ECONOMIC GROWTH IN FRANCE

At the turn of the century, after a depression that lasted from 1882 until 1897, the French economy was expanding. This expansion accounts for the general aura of prosperity in 1914 and for the nostalgic feelings for *la belle époque* that were prevalent after the war. But the rate of growth was less impressive than that of countries such as England, Germany, Belgium, and the United States. France, which had been second only to England in total industrial production in 1860, had dropped to fourth behind Germany and the United States in 1914. Between 1881 and 1885, the average annual income from the export of manufactured goods was $425,000,000 for France, $521,000,000 for Germany, and $1,113,000,000 for Britain. In the production of per capita real income, France stood behind the United States, England, Germany, Belgium, the Netherlands, Switzerland, and Sweden.

Historians offer a number of reasons for the relatively slow rate of economic growth in France between 1870 and 1914. Coal was in short supply, and the French had to import coal from abroad. In fact, 60 percent of French imports consisted of raw materials, and the value of her import of raw materials exceeded the value of her manufactured exports by 25 to 30 percent. Iron ore was the only industrial raw material that the country had in abundance. The high cost of transporting coal and other raw materials to the factories hindered industrial expansion. French capital that might have been invested in industry was invested instead in foreign enterprises and government bonds. Many Frenchmen hid their earnings in stockings under their beds or in buried strongboxes, which did not help the economy. The unequal distribution of wealth and income within the population weakened consumer power as did the existence at a subsistence level of a significant number of people. Other factors affecting economic growth include the effect of the government's protectionist policy on the modernization of industry as well as the attitude of the bourgeoisie toward economic activity. In 1914, French agriculture and industry were self-sustaining, even though tariffs and inefficient methods of production placed a greater burden on the consumer and even though France was lagging behind the more economically advanced nations.

THE ARISTOCRACY

The French aristocracy in the nineteenth century was even more heterogeneous than it had been during the Old Regime, when distinctions were made between the *noblesse d'epée,* the *noblesse de robe,* and the *noblesse de haute fonction.* The old aristocracy that traced its ancestry at least to the eighteenth century was joined by newer elements made up of the followers of the Bonapartists and Louis Philippe. These various groups had little in common. Most of them favored a regime other than the Republic; but, because they were unable to agree on an alternative, their political effectiveness was hampered.

Most aristocrats were religious. Some thought that the Catholic Church restored to the privileged position it had held before 1789 was essential to the spiritual and political well-being of the nation, and they applauded Pius IX's *Syllabus of Errors,* which refused to make concessions to the modern world. Others believed that the Church was important to the maintenance of moral order at a time of social upheaval, although they believed that Catholicism ought to make some concessions to post-revolutionary France. Many nobles, unable to pursue political careers under an alien regime, served their country in the Church or in the armed services. The Dreyfus affair was to reveal the extent to which the ideals and values of army officers and clergymen differed from the democratic ideals of many politicians and intellectuals.

The influence of the old aristocracy had steadily declined since the Revolution of 1830 when Charles X, who had intended to do all in his power to revive the Old Regime, was replaced by Louis Philippe. Many noblemen worked hard for the restoration of the Comte de Chambord but to no avail. Some legitimists transferred their allegiance to the Comte de Paris in 1883 when Chambord died without an heir, but others who could not put their trust in Orléanist princes decided instead to shift their allegiance to the Spanish Bourbons. Many members of the old aristocracy retired to their estates to live in peace with their memories, far removed from the modern world. Some legitimists continued to represent such counterrevolutionary regions as Brittany, the Vendée, and parts of Normandy in the Chamber and there they fought numerous rear-guard actions against Republicans. Only Albert De Mun from among Chambord's followers decided in 1893 to accept the established regime in obedience to his Church.

Orléanist and Bonapartist nobles were more worldly than the legitimists. Many of them had economic interests that caused them to be very much involved in the concerns of the moment. Some were captains of finance and industry. Others were large landowners who were interested in the latest agricultural developments. Orléanists and Bonapartists remained loyal to their respective houses as long as there was any reasonable expectation of a restoration. While some, including the Duc de Broglie and Marshal MacMahon, went to their graves hoping vainly for a change of regime, others came to the conclusion that they would have to accept the Republican form of government in order to protect their economic and social interests.

THE PEASANTS

The same variety that existed within the French peasantry in the eighteenth century was to be found at the end of the following century as well. There were prosperous farmers in the North and West who leased large tracts of land for a number of years; there were small landowners, sharecroppers, and day laborers, many of whom, particularly in the Midi and in the center, lived at a subsistence level, and who during the agricultural crisis were forced off the land. Until 1875, peasant life remained relatively unchanged. Rural communities were isolated, and approximately one third of the peasant population was illiterate.

Signs of change in rural life revealed themselves during the last two decades of the century. Railroads began to penetrate backward areas enabling farmers to become aware of a world beyond the village. Education was made available to a growing number of people, and the right to participate to some extent in political life was made secure with the firm establishment of universal manhood suffrage in 1871. When the agricultural crisis occurred, peasants were in a position to make use of their literacy, the ballot box, and the railroad to improve their condition. Peasants no longer able to eke out a living from the soil, as well as those for whom the drabness of rural life was no longer appealing, moved to other regions or to cities. After 1884, peasant cooperatives were established, first in order to buy badly needed fertilizers, but later in order to provide credit and insurance. These cooperatives helped to break down the narrow-minded individualism of the peasant and to prepare him for a more active role in the life of the community and of the nation. And the Third Republic was sensitive to their needs. The departmental councils that advised the prefects and elected senators gave the peasants the opportunity to make known their wishes, even though the peasants themselves did not go into politics either at the national or local level until the 1930s. They preferred instead to support nobles, lawyers, doctors, schoolteachers, and other *notables*.

The political views of the peasantry varied according to region and condition. The majority tended to support the regime of the moment, as long as that regime was capable of maintaining peace and prosperity. Hence the peasants supported the Second Empire until the Franco-Prussian War, but once the Third Republic revealed that it could maintain peace and that it too was interested in the condition of the peasantry, it received peasant support. There were, of course, exceptions to the general support of the regime, notably in the West where devotion to the aristocracy and to the Church resulted in peasant hostility to the Republic, and in the Northeast, the Southwest, and the Center where day laborers and small landowners were attracted to the appeal of revolutionary socialism.

THE BOURGEOISIE

The dominant social class in France after 1848 was the bourgeoisie, and the institutions of the Third Republic reflected many of the ideals and aspirations of that class. Yet analysis of the bourgeoisie reveals that it was made up of different interest groups often in conflict with each other. Ministerial instability during the Third Republic was in large part the result of tensions within the dominant social class. The political outlook and attitude of the village shopkeeper was obviously very different from the outlook and attitude of the Parisian banker.

The *haute bourgeoisie* consisted of bankers and industrialists, many of whom had acquired large fortunes and considerable social prestige. The concentration of economic power in the hands of a few financiers and industrialists appears at first glance to justify the Marxian claim that ultimately all power resides in the hands of a bourgeois oligarchy. This was not the case in France at the turn of the century because the economic and political interests of the *haute bourgeoisie* were often at variance with the interests of the Republic. Captains of finance and industry had become closely identified with Orléanism and Bonapartism, and they only reluctantly followed Thiers in 1873 and Jacques Piou in 1893 to accept the regime they never succeeded in dominating.

The *moyenne bourgeoisie,* numbering about three million, consisted of a number of interest groups. There were industrialists and merchants as well as members of the professional classes. Politics, and particularly the civil service, appealed to a growing number of middle-class youths; and, in an age when education was becoming important to all levels of society, a great many were attracted to the teaching profession. The lesser bourgeoisie, whose ranks merged with the *moyenne,* consisted of small shopkeepers, the lower echelons of the civil service, and white collar workers, a relatively new group that became prominent at the end of the century. The *moyenne* and *petite* bourgeoisie enthusiastically supported the Republic, which in return looked after their interests often at the expense both of big business and labor. The schoolteacher, the shopkeeper, and the subprefect were the Republic's shock troops at the grass roots in the struggle against the clergy and the aristocratic *notables.*

The bourgeoisie, in the Marxian scheme of things, is dominated by big business. Smaller enterprises are eventually swallowed up, being unable to compete with the larger units. The Marxists see bourgeois values as being derived from a society that has become industrialized and urbanized in contrast to aristocratic values that were derived from agrarian society. The Marxian conception of the bourgeoisie, fiercely competitive and entirely dominated by the profit motive, may have some relevance to the United States, Britain, and perhaps Germany at the end of the nineteenth century, but it has little relevance to France. The values of the French bourgeoisie were essentially traditional. Businesses were run on a small scale and were controlled by the family rather than by the *société anonyme*. Businessmen were more concerned about security than they were about limitless profit, and therefore French business methods were more often in the tradition of the guild system than in the newly established pattern of the monopolies and cartels of the United States and Germany. In the seventeenth century, Colbert complained that businessmen were investing too much capital in land and offices and too little in actual business enterprises. This complaint was somewhat valid in the nineteenth century, when French industrialists continued to buy estates and to retire from the world of affairs. The businessman was not as highly regarded in France as he was in the United States, perhaps because of a traditional French contempt for capitalist activity. The sons of the middle class were encouraged to pursue careers in politics, law, in the civil service, or at the university rather than in business. The educational system designed by and for the bourgeoisie stressed the humanities at the expense of the social sciences and technology. The French bourgeoisie like the peasantry was fundamentally conservative. Its values, to a remarkable extent, were shaped by the Old Regime despite the French and Industrial revolutions. It supported the Republic because the Republic shaped by Thiers had abandoned its revolutionary heritage in order to serve conservative interests.

THE INDUSTRIAL PROLETARIAT

The gradual expansion of French industry between 1870 and 1914 increased the size and importance of the industrial proletariat. On the eve of World War I, there were six million industrial workers in France. Toward the end of the century, the living conditions of the worker were improving as modern methods of production and transportation reduced the price of numerous commodities. At the same time, increased profits often meant higher salaries for the worker. Between 1870 and 1884, worker salaries in France rose 14 percent, while prices fell about the same amount. Living conditions were also improved because education was becoming more accessible and because the political and economic power of the workers was increasing with the right to vote and the right to organize trade unions. But, if the workers were better off at the end of the century than they had been in 1848, they were still not getting a fair share of the fruits of economic expansion. Life in the cities and factory towns continued to be harsh, as Émile Zola pointed up in his novels. The cost of living fluctuated, affecting the price of bread, so that if workers were no longer faced with abject poverty, they were still poor in comparison with other social groups. The mechanization of industry that accelerated after 1870 caused considerable dislocation within the working class. As they became aware of improved standards of living and as they developed political self-consciousness, workers set out to improve their position in French society.

After the Commune, the trade union movement in France suffered a serious setback, because its leaders were in prison or in exile and because the attitude of the government toward working-class organizations was extremely hostile. Nevertheless, after 1876, as the Republic became more secure, workers' co-operatives and mutual credit societies began to reappear; and, by 1881, there were 500 such organizations at the local level. In 1884, a law was passed under the auspices of the future Premier René Waldeck-Rousseau making trade unions entirely legal, but requiring registration of their constitutions, by-laws, and the names of their officers. In many cities throughout France, workers organized *Bourses du Travail*—or Labor Exchanges—in order to supply information about job opportunities and wages, and these became the focal point of the union movement. In 1892, a National Federation of *Bourses du Travail* was established; and, in 1902, all the workers' organizations in the country joined together to form the General Confederation of Labor (*Confédération Générale du Travail*) with membership of 600,000 workers in 1914. However, less than 5 percent of the French labor force was unionized at this time, because many workers were unaware of the movement, while others were prohibited by their employers from joining unions or frightened away by the militant attitude of the leaders of the CGT.

The theory and practice of trade unionism in France reflected the feelings of frustration and alienation experienced by many workers. Not only were employers hostile to unions, but most politicians were unsympathetic to labor's demands for a greater share of the national wealth. Union leaders were suspicious of the Socialists, who seemed to be constantly quarreling over doctrinal problems, and whose bourgeois origins made them a part of the hated "establishment."

The philosophy of the CGT is known as syndicalism, and its purpose was clearly defined in the Charter of Amiens in 1906: "The class struggle places the workers in revolt against all forms of capitalist exploitation and oppression, material and moral. . . . In its day-to-day demands, the union seeks . . . the increase of workers' well-being by the achievement of immediate gains, such as the shortening of hours, the raising of wages, and so forth. This effort, however, is only one side of the work of the union movement. It prepares for the complete emancipation of the worker which can be achieved only by expropriating the capitalist class." Most French Socialists shared the desire to overthrow capitalism, but they came to rely to an increasing extent on political action within the legal framework of the Republic. Syndicalism, on the other hand, emphasized direct action in the form either of riots or of the general strike, which would cause the entire capitalist structure to collapse. Violent action, as opposed to parliamentary debate, appealed to union leaders who regarded themselves as the guardians of the revolutionary tradition. The wave of strikes that occurred in France in the 1890s and early 1900s terrified many citizens who believed that another revolution was imminent, and it caused the government to respond with equal militancy to repress the strikes. By 1913, the revolutionary ardor of the CGT was considerably dampened by the use of troops against the workers and by the resistance of the employers to the demands of their employees. Recruiting fell off, and union leaders began to talk in more moderate terms. The decline of revolutionary syndicalism within the union movement made it easier for the CGT to cooperate with the Socialist Party, which had long since rejected the politics of violence.

CONCLUSION

French society at the end of the nineteenth century was essentially conservative, despite the revolutions of 1789, 1830, and 1848, in that it still retained many of the characteristics of the Old Regime. The old aristocracy, whose preeminent position was weakened throughout the century, still managed to retain social prestige; and, if its political power at the national level was negligible, it was strong in many rural areas. Its newer elements, Bonapartist and Orléanist, were deeply involved in the nation's economic development. And the peasants, whose attitude and outlook were shaped by centuries of attachment to the soil, played an important role in national affairs. No regime could afford to overlook the interests of the peasants. The values of the dominant class—the bourgeoisie—were traditional, having been derived in large part from the pre-revolutionary era. The French businessman was more interested in the security of his family than in the size of his profits, which might force him to take risks by investing capital in uncertain enterprises. Even the working class was conservatively inclined, in that many workers were reluctant to get involved in the revolutionary trade union movement.

The conservative nature of French society before World War I was reflected in the Republican regime, which distrusted strong government and protected conservative interests. The electoral system was so constructed as to give rural and agrarian interests a dominant voice in French politics at the local and national level. Efforts to give the cities and larger towns greater weight in the legislature and in the local councils were largely frustrated. The Méline tariff of 1892 helped to revive the national economy after the depression of the 1880s. Large and small farmers were able to sell their produce at a higher price when the threat of foreign competition was removed. Those who favored the tariff were thinking in terms of traditional agrarian interests, but they were not very concerned about the cost of protecting the urban consumer. The Méline tariff also protected industry from foreign competition; but, in so doing, it prevented industry from adopting techniques and new equipment that would have been useful to the future development of the country, both in terms of economic growth and in terms of cheaper production for the benefit of the consumer. In short, the Méline tariff provided a barrier not only to foreign commodities and produce, but also to modernization. French society was therefore protected against change; its population growth was negligible, its economic development was slow, and its political institutions were designed in large measure to protect vested interests.

3 / The Republic Endures, 1879–1899

THE FIRST ANTICLERICAL CAMPAIGN

The political history of the Third Republic between 1879 and 1899 divides itself into two periods. During the first ten years, the Republican majority in the National Assembly continued to grow at the expense of the anti-Republican Right; but, at the same time, disagreement on a number of issues within the majority made it increasingly ineffectual. During the decade between 1889 and 1899, an attempted realignment of political forces was based less on constitutional questions and more on economic and social problems.

The elections of 1881 were an overwhelming triumph for the Republicans. They returned to the Chamber of Deputies with a force of 378 members, while the Conservatives (the anti-Republican Right) were able to win only 90 seats. The only cloud on the horizon, from the Republican point of view, was the fact that the number of voters abstaining had never been so high. To the electorate, the Republic had become acceptable but not popular. In 1881, the Republicans appeared to be in a position to carry out any program they wanted. They had a Republican President, Jules Grévy, a Republican majority in the Senate, and a huge majority in the Chamber. But the elections of that year revealed that the Republicans disagreed on a number of important questions, and their disagreements were such that would make it very difficult for them to develop effective programs.

The majority of Republicans followed the popular Léon Gambetta, who had worked so hard to establish the regime in the 1870s. Gambetta had come to understand that politics consists of the art of the possible and that, unless Republicans compromised with hesitant Conservatives on a number of issues, there would be no Republic. In 1875, he and his supporters agreed to accept a President of the Republic and a bicameral legislature, even though this meant they were accepting those institutions that were to make the regime the conservative one that Adolphe Thiers sought. This desire to compromise was made very obvious in a speech that Gambetta delivered in 1881 insisting that the Republican program, including social legislation and the separation of church and state, would have to be carried out gradually. He was well aware of the deep political and social divisions that existed in his country, and he hoped that they would eventually be healed by a conciliatory Republican regime. It was for this reason that Gambetta's opponents called him an "opportunist," a label his followers would not be able to escape.

A minority of the Republicans in the 1880s—those who came to be known as Radicals—wanted an immediate enactment of the Republican program. On the eve of the elections of 1881, when Georges Clemenceau demanded that the presidency and the Senate be abolished and that the government of the Republic be entrusted to a unicameral legislature in the Jacobin tradition, he was stating the Radical position. Among his demands were the separation of church and state, the "right of the child to a complete education, lay, free, and compulsory," a progressive tax on capital, income, and inheritance as well as social legislation reducing the number of working hours, making employers responsible for workers' accidents, and legalizing trade unions. In fact, Clemenceau's social program impressed Karl Marx even though it did not impress many Republicans.

The role of the Catholic Church in French life was one issue upon which most Republicans could agree. Opportunists and Radicals were influenced to some extent by the positivist arguments of Auguste Comte and his disciples to the effect that progress depended upon a scientific understanding of natural laws rather than upon the Holy Spirit. In the tradition of the Enlightenment, Republicans insisted that the Catholic Church had misguided France for centuries. Only after its influence had been reduced to nothing could progress proceed unchecked and the Republic be secure. There were, of course, political reasons for the attack on the Church, arising from the close relationship between Catholicism and Conservativism.

Catholicism was in crisis in the nineteenth century because of the difficulty it had adjusting its authoritarian principles to liberal and democratic ideals. Some Catholics believed that Catholicism and liberalism were compatible, but the majority of the faithful agreed with Pius IX, who argued that freedom would destroy Christ's Church. Most French Catholics hoped for a restoration in 1871. Many put their trust in the Comte de Chambord to revive the intimate connection between throne and altar. The Comte de Paris and the Orléanists also showed themselves to be friends of the Church as did the Bonapartists, most of whom believed that the impieties of Napoleon I had been compensated for by his nephew's assistance to the Vatican and by the devotion of the Empress Eugénie. Few Catholics agreed with Lammenais that the Catholic Church would flourish under a democratic Republic.

When the Republic was firmly established in 1879, the power and influence of the Church was still considerable. Priests campaigned for Monarchist politicians, the officer corps was solidly Catholic, and the French educational system was very much subjected to religious influence. Napoleon I had done much to secularize education at all levels; and, as a result of his efforts, two systems, Catholic and public, existed side by side from the primary school to the university. Between 1815 and 1879, the Church gradually had increased its control over the public schools. The successive regimes of the period had made this possible because they were sympathetic to the Church, because they believed that the Church should exert a strong moral influence in times of social crisis, or because the Church was capable of providing more teachers than the state. In 1879, there were many villages with only Catholic schools, and there were villages and towns where priests and bishops sat on local school boards and taught in public schools. All secondary education for girls was in the hands of the Church. The universities were imbued with the spirit of positivism and hence free from Catholic influence; but, in 1875, the Church received from the Monarchist Assembly the right to establish its own institutions of higher learning. The only restriction placed upon them was that they be called institutes rather than universities, a distinction that continues to exist.

The anticlerical campaign that the Republicans undertook in 1879 was the result of a combination of forces—the influence of positivism, the realization that democracy and nineteenth century Catholicism were incompatible, and the conviction that young French citizens would become loyal to the regime only if Catholic influence on the schools was sharply curtailed. Anticlericalism was an issue that joined most Republicans in agreement. The chief strategist of the campaign was Jules Ferry, a colorless but extremely capable Opportunist who was to dominate the political scene from 1881 to 1885. In 1879, as Minister of Education, Ferry sponsored a bill that denied the right of Catholic schools to issue degrees and that contained the famous "Article Seven" barring unauthorized religious orders from teaching in public or private schools. Since all the Catholic teaching orders were "unauthorized" by the Concordat of 1801 (although they usually had been tolerated since then), Article Seven would have caused a severe shortage of teachers in the primary and secondary schools. The article was defeated in the Senate because it offended liberal sentiments as well as the Catholic sensibilities.

The Republican majority in the Chamber immediately retaliated by demanding that the government enforce the provisions of the Concordat. In 1882, a law was passed that prohibited religious instruction in the schools, replacing it with civic instruction. Subsequent legislation in 1886 stipulated that members of Catholic orders would be permitted to teach in public schools for only five more years, after which time it was assumed that the state teachers' colleges would be able to produce replacements. In that same legislation, money was provided by the Chamber to construct public schools for girls. Other laical laws of the period included repeal of the Sunday rest law in 1880, the reinstatement of civil marriage and divorce, the removal of crucifixes from courtrooms, the subjection of seminarians to military service (*curés-sac-au-dos*), and the reestablishment of the Parisian Church of Ste. Geneviève as the "Pantheon," the shrine of the Republic.

Opportunists and Radicals disagreed on the question of separation of church and state. The Radicals thought that the Concordat of 1801 gave the Church too much political influence, but the Opportunists maintained that the Concordat provided the government with a means of controlling the activity of the Church. Bishops and priests who attacked the regime too vehemently were liable to have their salaries suspended, and the government had some voice in the selection of bishops. Separation, from the Opportunist point of view, meant freeing the Church, thereby enabling her more easily to subvert the state. As long as the Opportunists dominated the ministries, the Concordat was to remain intact.

The laical legislation enacted in the 1880s was not designed entirely to destroy the influence of Catholicism. It also provided free, compulsory education at the primary level for all Frenchmen, a requisite that was considered to be both indispensable to the proper functioning of democracy and in keeping with the general educational trend of western Europe and the United States, despite its being inimical to the interests of the Church. However, the Church did continue to wield some influence within the public school system because of the inability of the teachers' colleges to produce the necessary number of teacher replacements. The laical law had a profound effect upon the nation as a whole. Despite Gambetta's hope that it would be conciliatory, the Republic developed a rigid orthodoxy and exclusiveness that only served to accentuate political differences.

Catholics who had proved their loyalty to the Republic in the crisis of *seize mai* were shut out.

GAMBETTA AND FERRY

The Third Republic was not attracted to strong leaders, as can be seen by the election of Jules Grévy to the presidency in 1879. Gambetta was an attractive figure with obvious political appeal, but his political career was affected adversely by this predilection for weaklings. In the autumn of 1870, when he had tried and failed to organize victory over the Prussians, Gambetta had assumed virtual dictatorial powers. He was largely responsible for mobilizing support for the Republic in the 1870s and was a natural candidate for election to the presidency in 1879, but his leadership qualities were his undoing. With the success of Grévy, Gambetta was the obvious choice to be his first Premier; but Grévy preferred the average to the extraordinary, and he feared that Gambetta's prestige might corrupt the Republic into becoming another Consulate. Although Gambetta had a genuine desire to compromise, his inflammatory and revolutionary language disguised this fact and frightened his colleagues.

In 1881, after the overwhelming victory of the Republicans at the polls, Grévy was no longer able to ignore Gambetta, whom he asked to form a government. Gambetta hoped to form a government of national union, a "ministry of all the talents," and he announced his intention of offering portfolios to several former premiers, but they all, for a variety of reasons, refused his advances. Gambetta's ministry, as it evolved, consisted of a number of bright young men with reputations yet to be made. And hoping to please Conservatives, the Premier made some concessions in appointments in the army, the administration, and the diplomatic corps. Sensing that his enemies were waiting for the right moment to bring down the government, Gambetta proposed a number of reforms that included weakening the power of the Senate (a move designed to please the Radicals) and a return to the *scrutin de liste,* which he hoped would make political parties more homogeneous and more disciplined. Immediately, his opponents accused him of Caesarism; and, after three months in office, the "ministry of all the talents" was overthrown. A few months later, Gambetta died, and the Republican politicians—who preferred their heroes dead—honored him by burying his heart in the Pantheon and reviving the *scrutin de liste.*

Jules Ferry, who succeeded Gambetta as the de facto leader of the Opportunists, met with a similar political fate. The chief architect of the laical laws, he was also largely responsible for the imperial expansion of France in Asia and North Africa. Ferry was detested by Conservatives and by Radicals and others who felt that France's empire weakened her position on the European continent, making her more vulnerable to Germany. Ferry headed two governments: the first, in 1881, fell after a few months, but the second lasted from 1883 until 1885, a long time for a government during the Third Republic. When his second government was brought down in March 1885 as a result of French military action against China, Ferry had become one of the least liked men in France. This was in part because he was a competent administrator. When, in 1886, the Republic had the opportunity to elect Ferry to the presidency, it chose instead the ineffectual Sadi-Carnot, grandson of a distinguished Republican leader, pointing up once again its preference for honoring the dead rather than the living.

THE BOULANGER CRISIS

The elections of 1885 reflected the considerable frustration and dissatisfaction prevalent in France at that time. The economic depression affected both agriculture and industry by 1882. Large and small landowners saw land values fall and rents collapse; peasants in the Midi were forced off the land into the cities; and the industrial recession caused widespread unemployment. Many *notables* and peasants were seething from the anticlerical legislation, and patriotic citizens were outraged at the government's imperialist policy and the decline of the revanchist spirit. These dissatisfactions, in the face of the elections of 1885, constituted a threat to the Republic. On the first ballot, the Republicans polled approximately 4,100,000 popular votes to the Conservatives' 3,500,000. However, they received 127 seats in the Chamber, compared with 176 seats for the Conservatives. The future of the regime depended upon the second ballot a week later. Their discipline during the election campaign saved the day for the Republicans; the new Chamber consisted of 383 Republicans and 201 Conservatives.

In 1885, the Conservatives, who in 1881 had been a negligible political force, were able to form a common front—a *union des droites*—something they had been unable to do earlier. In 1883, the Comte de Chambord had died; and Monarchists, with a few exceptions, were able to unite behind his political heir, the Comte de Paris. The Bonapartists within the Conservative ranks refused to follow the Orléanist pretender, but they were unable themselves to agree on who should succeed the Prince Imperial, who had died in Africa in 1878 (Prince Jerome Bonaparte and his son Victor were the two rival candidates.) Unable to agree on constitutional questions, the Conservatives did manage to agree on economic and religious matters, and it was on this basis that they formed the *union des droites*. They produced a program that called for an end to religious persecution and a reduction in public spending. Even this degree of party unity at a time when Opportunists and Radicals were squabbling was sufficient to revive the political fortunes of the Right. Between 1871 and 1873, the Republicans had been able to take advantage of Conservative disunity to advance the cause of the Republic, and now in 1885 the tables were turned. But, until the Right could agree on constitutional questions, its opportunities were limited.

After the elections of 1885, the aura of discontent continued to hang heavy over France. The economic crisis deepened, and the Republic seemed unable to provide effective leadership. What leadership it did have suffered from a scandal in 1886. President Grévy's son-in-law, Senator Daniel Wilson, had considerable political influence, including the power to recommend appointments, awards, and decorations, and he was inclined to bestow his recommendations upon those who were willing to pay for the honor. When Wilson was discovered, the President of the Republic was placed in a very embarrassing position, not only because he was close to his son-in-law but also because Wilson conducted his business from the President's own residence, the Elysée Palace. Grévy quite naturally disassociated himself from Wilson in a desperate effort to hold on to his office. But public opinion was in no mood to tolerate corruption in high places. The former communard Henri de Rochefort conducted a vicious campaign against the President in his popular newspaper, *La Lanterne;* and Conservatives, eager to discredit the regime whenever the opportunity presented itself, pressed for Grévy's resignation. The President fought desperately to hold on to his office, but the threat of a parliamentary strike finally dislodged him. He was unable to form a ministry because no one would accept a portfolio unless he resigned, which he did in November 1886. It was shortly thereafter that Sadi-Carnot was elected to succeed him.

In this atmosphere of discontent, General Boulanger appeared to perform the function of a badly needed hero. This man on horseback was trained as an officer at Saint-Cyr, the French military academy, had served in Africa and Indo-China before returning to France to be wounded and promoted in the defense of Paris. (It was fortunate for him that he was not involved in the massacre of the communards.) During the early stages of his career, General Boulanger was Catholic and Conservative; but, when he saw that the Third Republic was firmly established, he accepted it enthusiastically as the surest means of advancement. He and the Radical Clemenceau had been classmates at the lycée at Nantes, and it was as a friend of the Radicals that Boulanger came forward into the center of the political arena.

In response to the significant gains of the Radicals in the elections of 1885, which entitled them to ministerial positions, Boulanger was invited to become Minister of War in the third

Freycinet ministry. Handsome and energetic, he immediately set out to make the most of his position and his personality. He initiated a number of reforms, including improved standards of cleanliness and comfort, and saw to it that morale remained high by encouraging *esprit de corps* so badly needed after the great defeat of 1870. He followed the Radical program of republicanizing the officer corps by removing those who were blatantly royalist from positions of command. (He infuriated his future Conservative supporters by taking a command away from the exceedingly capable Duc D'Aumale, the son of Louis Philippe.)

General Boulanger was a welcome sight to that small minority who still dreamed of a war of revenge against Germany. Paul Déroulède was one of those fanatic patriots who hoped to return Alsace and Lorraine to France but who dispaired of the colorless Republic's ever doing anything about it, and he founded the League of Patriots in the hope of sustaining the revanchist spirit and revising the constitution along authoritarian lines. To Déroulède, Boulanger seemed to be the answer to France's problems. The Radical general excited Parisian crowds when he led military parades, and his great popularity was seen further in the number of patriotic songs composed by the songwriter Paulus. The Minister of War's military reforms—which included better weapons—attracted Bismarck's attention, prompting the German Chancellor to undertake military preparations on a fairly large scale. (Bismarck was also anxious to pass a septennial military law through the Reischstag and thought that a little saber-rattling might help.) The Chancellor called Boulanger a menace to peace, which titillated French patriots but which caused others to become alarmed at the mounting tension between the two states.

An incident occurred in April 1887 when a French espionage agent, Schnaebelé, was arrested on German soil. An indignant outcry arose in France when it was learned that the spy had been lured across the border by German police, and Boulanger demanded partial mobilization. When Bismarck discovered that Schnaebelé was covered by a safe-conduct letter to meet German officials, he ordered his release, to the delight of French patriots. Despite Boulanger's popularity, many of the Republican politicians, aware that France was unprepared for war, realized that the general was irresponsible and worked to get him out of the ministry. When Boulanger, who was not a candidate, almost won a by-election in Paris, even his Radical friends became alarmed. Boulanger had become the darling of the crowds of Paris, but his popularity was seen as a danger to the Republic. In 1887, the new Rouvier ministry excluded Boulanger, much to his chagrin, and assigned him command of the 13th Army Corps at Clermont-Ferrand. When he departed from the Gare de Lyons on July 8, hysterical Parisians shouted "To the Elysée!"

The second act of the Boulanger drama began in late 1887. The general was still sulking in the provinces over Republican fickleness, but Conservatives were coming to the conclusion that the former Minister of War might be of use to them. The Right had staged a dramatic comeback in the elections of 1885, but it still had little political influence. Monarchists had been infuriated in 1886 when the heads of former French ruling families were exiled after a lavish wedding given his daughter by the Comte de Paris. This wedding was viewed by the government, whose members had not been invited, as a Monarchist demonstration. Conservatives decided that Boulanger might be the means whereby the Right could force a revision of the constitution. In the summer of 1887, the general met Prince Jerome Bonaparte at the latter's home on the shores of Lake Geneva, where both agreed on a program that would involve constitutional revision, a plebiscite (a favorite Bonapartist tactic), and the establishment of a regime with a strong executive. Boulanger received Napoleon's sword but no money. In September 1887, the Comte de Paris helped the Boulanger cause by announcing from England that he, too, favored a plebiscite.

General Boulanger now had a great deal of support from the Right as well as from the extreme Left, where urban workers and peasants, hard hit by the depression, looked to him for relief. He also had financial resources supplied to him through

Arthur Meyer, editor of the conservative *Gaulois*. His chief backers were the Duchesse D'Uzès and the Jewish banker Baron Hirsch, and his campaign manager was a Franco-Irish noble, Count Dillon, who had spent time in the United States and had learned something about American electioneering tactics. A number of newspapers—including Rochefort's *L'Intransigeant,* the *Gaulois, L'Univers,* and the newly established *La Cocarde*—lent Boulanger support.

Boulangist politics, as it developed, involved entering the general in as many by-elections as possible with a necessarily vague platform calling for the dissolution of the Chamber and the summoning of a constitutional assembly to be charged with revising the constitution. Eventually, his followers hoped to cause the collapse of the regime by pressuring it with the Boulangist electoral victories. The government responded to the general's involvement in politics by dismissing him from the army entirely.

The Boulangist campaign throughout 1888 was extremely successful. The general won a number of by-elections in Bonapartist and clerical strongholds, as well as in the industrial North where worker discontent was prevalent. Multiple candidacies were permitted during the early years of the Republic, which enabled Boulanger to present himself as a candidate as many times as he desired. The climax of the campaign occurred when the government decided to force a showdown with Boulanger in Paris, where a parliamentary vacancy had recently opened up. The election was fixed for January 27, 1889; and the Republicans rallied behind one candidate, a M. Jacques, who entered the lists against "General Revanche." All the financial resources that the government could bring to bear in support of the official candidate were matched by funds from the Duchesse D'Uzès' treasury, and Boulanger won the election easily.

The wildly enthusiastic crowds that had toppled so many regimes and now appeared to have turned against the Third Republic gathered in the Place de la Madeleine to press for a *coup d'état*. The moment of truth for the former Minister of

War came and went very quickly. Boulanger was not a revolutionary, and he could not bring himself to act illegally. Despite the urging of his lieutenants to move against the Elysée Palace, he preferred to spend the night with his mistress, Madame De Bonnemains. The government now had the opportunity to pull itself together and to launch a counteroffensive.

Boulangism collapsed very quickly after January 27. The tough, able Minister of the Interior, Ernest Constans, decided to frighten the general by having it rumored that Boulanger was about to be arrested for treasonable activities, a charge which could not possibly stick. The darling of the Parisian crowds showed his true colors by escaping to Belgium with his mistress, thereby embarrassing his followers and destroying the movement. In 1891, a few weeks after Madame De Bonnemains died of consumption in Brussels, Boulanger committed suicide on her grave. His old friend Clemenceau suggested as an epitaph: "Here lies General Boulanger who died, as he had lived, a subaltern."

The Boulangist movement was the product of a number of forces that came together in the 1880s to endanger the Republic. There was the feeling held by many that the regime was colorless and dull and that it was incapable of coping with crisis. Urban workers and peasants came to believe that little was being done by the government to help them in time of distress. Hard times in France in the nineteenth century had caused popular sentiment to become antagonistic to whatever regime happened to be in power. The Right saw in Boulanger the opportunity of capitalizing on their success of 1885, and they supported the man whom they hoped would make constitutional revision popular. They never made clear what kind of revision it would be because of the divisions within the Right and because of the heterogeneous nature of the general's support. Boulangism was in part the product of the frustrated nationalism that motivated Paul Déroulède and the League of Patriots, and it was also in part the result of a fear of Germany constantly present in the hearts of many Frenchmen—a fear aggravated by Bismarck's saber-rattling in 1887. If the Bou-

langist leadership came mostly from the Right, the popular
support came from the Left. The crowds in the Place de la
Madeleine on January 27, 1889, were imbued with the old Jacobin spirit that thrived on economic hardship and on an instinc-
tive fear that the country was in danger.

The short and long term consequences of the movement
were considerable. The Conservatives had gambled on the man
on horseback and lost much of the ground gained in 1885. The
elections of September 1889, an anticlimax after the excitement
of January, returned 166 Republicans to the Chamber. Although
the complexion of the lower house had not changed much since
the previous elections, Conservative politicians were demoralized
and faced with the choice of either futile agitation against a
Republic that was more strongly entrenched than ever or ad-
hering to the regime. Republicans emerged successfully from
the recent elections satisfied that the Republic had endured,
but they were plagued by internecine squabbles. The Boulanger
crisis revealed, however, that there was still a strong anti-parlia-
mentarian, authoritarian tendency reminiscent of Bonapartism
in the country—a tendency that was attractive to both conservative and radical elements, that had appeared with every political and social crisis since 1789, and that if suppressed in 1889
would reappear in other crises in the future.

THE *RALLIEMENT*

The Republic had survived a serious challenge to its existence during the decade between 1879 and 1889. The question of
the nature of the regime, so important during the Boulangist
campaign, became significantly less important after 1889 when
pressing problems arising out of the depression, urbanization, and
industrialization came to the fore. The sense of political frustration prevalent in the 1880s was accentuated in the 1890s by the
terrorist activity of the anarchists and by the growing appeal of
syndicalism within the working class. On March 11, 1892, a young
man threw a bomb in the Boulevard St. Germain in Paris; and,
on December 9, 1893, another threw a bomb in the Chamber,

wounding a deputy. On February 12, 1894, another explosive was tossed into the Gare St. Lazare in Paris, killing one person and wounding twenty more. However, the most dramatic *attentat* perpetrated by the anarchists occurred in Lyons on June 24, 1894, when an Italian, Santo Cesario, jumped into the carriage of Sadi-Carnot and stabbed the President of the Republic to death. The *Ralliement* (the effort to rally Conservatives to the Republic) and the rise of socialism must be regarded as efforts on the part of the French body politic to come to grips with social problems that were made more urgent by the appeals to violence by groups on the extreme Left.

The *Ralliement* resulted from the failure of the Right to play an effective role in French politics after 1877 and from the inability of the Boulangist movement to force constitutional revision along lines appealing to Conservatives. On March 21, 1890, a Monarchist deputy, Jacques Piou, founded an organization that called itself the *Droite constitutionnelle* (the constitutional Right), consisting of a number of Conservative deputies who had reluctantly come to the conclusion that they would have to accept the Republican form of government. These men were mostly large landowners and industrialists who were feeling the effects of the depression and who believed that the time had come to set aside futile constitutional questions and to adjust their politics to suit their economic interests.

While Piou was attempting to change the course of Conservative politics, Pope Leo XIII was in the process of concluding that Catholic interests would best be served by coming to terms with the Third Republic. On November 12, 1890, one of the most influential French cardinals, Lavigerie, Primate of North Africa, gave a dinner for the officers of a French naval squadron at Algiers, at which he stated in a toast that French Catholics, in the interests of social order, ought to accept the Republic despite the laical legislation. The officers were horrified by the toast as were many other conservatives, who tried to persuade themselves that the cardinal was speaking for himself and not for the Church; but there was little doubt that Lavigerie's speech had been inspired by the Pope, who eventually issued an encyclical—*Au milieu des sollicitudes*—calling for Catholic acceptance of the legally established form of government.

Despite the efforts of Piou, Lavigerie, and Leo XIII to rally Catholics and Conservatives to the Republic, they were only partially successful. Many Monarchists and Bonapartists were too emotionally committed to their respective dynasties to become Republicans, and many Catholics were convinced that the regime would always be dominated by Jews, Protestants, and Freemasons. The *Droite constitutionnelle,* consisting mainly of former Orléanists and Bonapartists, urged the formation of a homogeneous conservative party that would include Republicans and would protect private property; and, before the elections of 1892, it announced that it would support any Republican government that energetically resisted the socialist menace. In 1893, 36 *ralliés* were elected, along with 58 intransigent Conservatives. At the same time, 49 Socialists were returned to the Chamber.

Leo XIII was not discouraged by the refusal of intransigent Catholics and Conservatives to heed his advice. In January 1896, he summoned the Catholic Republican Étiènne Lamy to Rome with the intention of making him the political leader of French Catholic forces. Lamy's organization, the *Fédération électorale,* attempted to promote unity among French Catholics and to bring support to a conservative Republic at a time when revolutionary elements seemed to be dominating the Left. Lamy came up against the same problem that Piou had encountered before 1893. Many Catholic leaders would not compromise with Republican politicians, despite the "social question." The most influential and popular Catholic order, the Assumptionist Fathers—whose newspaper, *La Croix,* had a large circulation—succeeded in sabotaging Lamy's plans for the elections of 1898. These plans had called for cooperation with the Opportunists in spite of the laical legislation, and the *Ralliement* suffered the same fate at the polls in 1898 that it had in 1893. There were too many Monarchists and Catholics for whom economic and social questions were of less importance than the nature of the regime.

The success of the *Ralliement* depended not only upon Conservative attitudes but also upon the attitudes of Opportunists.

Gambetta's followers were not blind to the needs of the unfortunate people affected by depression and industrialization. Opportunist governments between 1881 and 1899 had brought about the enactment of a good deal of legislation favorable to the working class, including the legal recognition of trade unions, reduction of the number of working hours of women and children, employer liability for accidents at work, and in 1891 the beginnings of a project that would provide workers' pensions. But as the Socialist movement gained momentum in the 1890s, Opportunists became increasingly committed to a policy of social order and to Thiers' conception of a conservative Republic. They would have liked to govern France on their own; but, as the Radicals continued to gain seats in the Chamber after the elections of 1885, it became apparent to Gambettists that they would have to seek outside support to maintain a parliamentary majority. At first, the Opportunists sought Radical support, despite the differences that plagued the Republican factions, but this made it difficult for ministries that were formed on the basis of compromise to adopt resolute policies of social order. In the 1890s, many Radicals, paying heed to the principle that they should have no enemies on the Left, were sympathetic to the Socialist movement. This alarmed Opportunists, some of whom came to agree with the *Droite constitutionnelle* on the need for a conservative Republican party based on the maintenance of social order and the protection of private property.

In order to accept the basic premise of the *Ralliement,* the Opportunists had to overcome their anticlerical instincts, which was difficult for them to do. They had been pleased by the Lavigerie toast and by the papal encyclical but were skeptical of the ability of Conservatives to become Republicans. For this reason they did not cooperate with the *Droite constitutionnelle* during the electoral campaign of 1893. At the same time, however, they fought Radical candidates with increasing vigor, and this brought about Clemenceau's defeat in the election of that year. But a bomb in the Chamber in December 1893 and the increase in the number of Socialist seats succeeded in making some Opportunists more receptive to the *Ralliement.*

On March 3, 1894, the Minister of Public Worship, an old associate of Gambetta and former editor of the Opportunist newspaper *La République Française* Eugène Spuller, made a speech in the Chamber calling for a "new spirit" of reconciliation between Republicans and Conservatives as a means of defending the social order. This *ésprit nouveau* seemed to be realized between April 1896 and June 1898, when Jules Méline headed an Opportunist ministry. This former lieutenant of Gambetta's had been primarily responsible for the revival of protectionism, which culminated in the Méline tariff of 1892. Large landowners and industrialists, many of whom were *ralliés,* benefited from high tariffs, and they willingly gave their support to Méline. In the campaign of 1898, the Méline ministry discreetly cooperated with *ralliés,* thereby indicating that it was amenable to the idea of forming a conservative Republican party. There were, however, Opportunists such as Louis Barthou and Raymond Poincaré who, like the intransigent Conservatives, were unwilling to forget their political heritage in the interests of the *Ralliement.* Opportunists were as divided as Conservatives, and this doomed the movement initiated by Jacques Piou and Leo XIII.

The *Ralliement* was a significant development because it indicated that the Catholic Church was trying to come to terms with the modern world and that the liberal Catholic position, which sought to endorse principles that had emerged from the French Revolution, was valid. In fact Etiènne Lamy's *Fédération électorale* was an attempt to implement liberal Catholic ideals. If the movement failed to convince many Conservative politicians, it did bring many Catholics to vote for Republican candidates in the elections of 1893 and 1898. The *Ralliement* was significant because it tried, if unsuccessfully, to focus the attention of French conservatism on economic and social rather than on constitutional issues and to bring about an alliance between the Opportunists and the Right. What it did succeed in doing was to damage the anti-Republican Right and to cause such a split in the ranks of the Opportunists as to end the political hegemony of the group that had dominated the ministries since 1879.

FRENCH SOCIALISM

The emergence of Socialism as a political force in the 1890s showed that a realignment of political forces was taking place on the Left as well as on the Right. The French Socialist movement had been badly hurt by the repressive actions taken by the government after the Commune had been crushed. The Dufaure Law of 1872 had outlawed the First International, and many Socialist leaders were either in exile or in hiding. Once the Republic was solidly established, Socialist activity was permitted, and the economic depression of the 1880s stimulated the movement. Socialist principles in France were derived from a number of sources, which helps to explain why there were so many internal disputes between 1870 and 1905 when the French Socialist Party was founded. Auguste Blanqui, one of the founders who owed much to the Jacobin tradition, had stressed the importance of violent revolutionary action under the leadership of an intellectual elite, a view that later appealed to Lenin. Pierre-Joseph Proudhon, whose influence on the Socialist movement up through the Commune of 1871 was particularly strong, emphasized the importance of a community in which labor would control the means of production and in which the need for political institutions would be minimal. His vision of France made up of loosely federated communes owed something to Rousseau and French provincialism. Unlike most Socialists who in true nineteenth-century fashion regarded the state as evil, Louis Blanc, another of the movement's founders, saw in the state the means whereby Socialist aims could be realized. The impact of Marxism on the French Socialist movement occurred in the 1860s; and, under the Third Republic, the movement became increasingly influenced by Marxian principles.

The leading Marxist in France in the 1880s was Jules Guesde. In 1871, he had fled to Switzerland to escape a prison sentence imposed on him for his support of the Commune. Returning to his country in 1876, he founded a newspaper,

L'Égalité, in order to expound Marxist principles; and in 1882, he helped found the French Workers' Party. The working class, he believed, ought to have a party that would develop a consciousness of the tasks assigned to it by history and would prepare for the proletarian revolution. Under no circumstances should the Workers' Party cooperate with bourgeois parties within the legal framework, because that framework was constructed to promote bourgeois interests. In the 1880s, a group of Socialists rejected the idea that no social reform could occur before the proletarian revolution took place and stressed the importance of working for piecemeal legislation within the legal framework and of cooperating with bourgeois parties if necessary. These possibilists applied to socialism the same principles that Gambetta had applied to Republicanism. In 1891, a number of dissident possibilists, led by the typesetter Jean Allemane, tried to find a middle ground between reformist and revolutionary socialism by pointing out the efficacy of any action legal or extra-legal that might help the cause.

The man who had the most profound effect on French socialism before 1914, and who devoted all his effort to reconciling the various conflicting elements within the movement, was Jean Jaurès. He was born in the Tarn, a mining region greatly affected by the Industrial Revolution, and he was educated at the elite *École Normale Superieure.* Jaurès began his career as a philosophy professor at a provincial high school, but he soon became attracted to politics and was elected to the Chamber in 1885 as an Opportunist. Aware that the Republicans were not doing enough to resolve social problems, Jaurès became a Socialist. He accepted the Marxist concept of a revolution that would destroy the capitalist system, but he rejected the Marxist belief that men's actions were determined by impersonal historic forces, preferring instead to emphasize the moral impulse that made men want to create a harmonious society. Jaurès' brilliant mind, his attractive personality, and his prowess as an orator made him not only a great Socialist leader but also one of the Third Republic's outstanding leaders.

The elections of 1893 returned 49 Socialists of varying shades and opinions to the Chamber, including Jaurès and Guesde. Both continued to regard themselves as "revolutionary Socialists," but they rejected violence and syndicalism in favor of the peaceful transformation of society. Instead, they counted on the disciplined action of the Socialist Party and the support of an electorate increasingly aware of the evils of capitalism to cause such a transformation. Where the Guesdists differed from the Jaurèssians was in their attitude toward cooperating with bourgeois parties and in their attitude toward the Republic. According to the Guesdists, Socialists should remain in perpetual opposition until they were in a position to dominate the regime, which they would then revise according to Marxist principles. Jaurès believed that the Republic embodied the great revolutionary tradition, but he wanted to "socialize" it—with the cooperation of other groups if necessary.

Alexandre Millerand, one of the Socialist leaders, gave a speech at a banquet in the Parisian suburb of St. Mandé, where leaders of the various Socialist factions were celebrating important gains in the local elections of 1896. His St. Mandé program called upon the state "to convert from capitalist into national property the different categories of the means of production and exchange in proportion as they become ripe for social appropriation." He called for the triumph of socialism through the democratic process made available by the Republic, and he demanded the formation of an international workers' organization. Most Socialists agreed with this program but disagreed on the means of implementing it. The presence of a fairly large group of Socialists in the Chamber accentuated the problem of whether to work within the legal framework in cooperation with other groups or to remain in permanent opposition.

French socialism in the 1890s had to contend not only with its relationship with the Republic and Republican parties but also its relationship with workers and peasants. Guesde and Jaurès wanted a Socialist Party that was primarily a workers' party, but worker sentiment reflected in the trade union movement was suspicious of bourgeois intellectuals who claimed that they were on the side of the proletariat and was distrustful of the reformist tendency, which sought cooperation with a regime that from the union point of view was becoming more conservative in the 1890s. Despite the efforts of Socialist leaders to achieve social legislation and despite their appearance at strikes, the CGT remained at arm's length from the Socialist movement during the last decade of the nineteenth century. From the Socialist point of view, the peasant problem was vexing because Marx and others had sought to collectivize agriculture. The French peasant, however, was attached to his small farm even though it did not afford him much of a living. Jaurès, who came from a region where farmers were poor, was well aware of their grievances and their commitment to private ownership. French socialism, therefore, came to defend traditional small ownership as French agriculture moved away from it, thereby providing another example of the conservative or traditional influence on French politics.

The same concern for the effects of economic developments on the lower classes that stimulated Socialist activity in the 1880s also stimulated the charitable instincts of a number of French Catholics. In the 1870s, two ardent Monarchists, Albert de Mun and the Marquis de la Tour du Pin, had established "workers' circles" (*Oeuvres des cercles*) designed to study problems of immediate interest to workers and to promote cooperation between employers and employees. Catholic interest in the social problems generated by the accelerated pace of the Industrial Revolution was made explicit in Leo XIII's great encyclical, *Rerum novarum*, which among other things admitted the right of the state to interfere in the economic order to improve the condition of the working class. Inspired by the *Oeuvres des cercles* and by *Rerum novarum*, a number of young priests and laymen in the 1890s decided to promote social democratic principles that they believed to be compatible with the Catholic tradition. The Christian Democratic movement, designed to bring the Church back to the people, had relatively little success because the proletariat was thoroughly alienated from Catholicism and because workers were suspicious of the paternalist attitude of some priests and

laymen. It had some small success in the North, where the Abbé
Lemire was elected as a Christian Democrat in 1893, but the
chief significance of the movement is that it reflected the extent
to which Frenchmen of varying backgrounds and traditions had
become troubled by the "social question."

THE PANAMA SCANDAL AND THE DREYFUS AFFAIR

Just as the French body politic was trying to reject futile
constitutional questions and to adjust to economic and social
circumstances, it was jolted by a scandal and a crisis that inter-
fered with this process and caused many to conclude that the
Republic was in danger once again.

Ferdinand de Lesseps, the engineer who had built the Suez
Canal, organized the Panama Company in 1880 to construct a
canal through the isthmus of Panama. Because of his previous
success, de Lesseps had no difficulty in attracting small investors,
whom he preferred to the large banks that would be inclined to
hamper operations by constantly demanding accounts of cost.
But like the Mississippi Company organized by John Law in 1717
to exploit Louisiana and resolve the financial crisis confronting
the Old Regime, the Panama project was poorly conceived and
poorly organized. Enormous sums of money were consumed in
the mud and jungle, and yellow fever made it difficult to organize sufficient manpower. The two men chiefly responsible
for public relations and for raising money were Jacques de
Reinach and Dr. Cornelius Herz. The precarious situation of the
company was hidden from the public by bribing newspapermen
and politicians, but the company finally went bankrupt in 1889.

In 1892, pressure from the press and public opinion eventually forced the Chamber to begin an investigation into the company's operations, and the sordid story of bribes and payoffs
unfolded. Reinach committed suicide; Herz fled to England; de
Lesseps and his son were tried and given prison sentences;
in the elections of 1893, the voters had a chance to punish
some of the politicians involved. Clemenceau, whose newspaper

Justice received money from Herz and who cooperated with the company to keep it from sinking, was one of those who lost his seat.

The entire savings of many investors were wiped out because of the company's failure, a fact which further irritated the general economic condition of the country. Conservatives who did not wish to heed Jacques Piou's appeal to rally to the regime took great pleasure in pointing out how corrupt the Republic was, and the Socialists were able to take advantage of the scandal by winning a number of seats in the Chamber using the same argument. Anti-Semitism, which was beginning to emerge as a significant force in Europe at the end of the century, thrived on the misdeeds of Reinach and Herz, both Jews. Although the regime was in no way threatened by the scandal, it was tarnished by it and consequently more vulnerable to the vitriolic attacks of its enemies during the Dreyfus affair.

The anti-Semitic *Libre Parole* announced in October 1894 that a Jewish officer had been arrested for espionage; and the French press, which was to play such an important role in the affair, began to agitate for a speedy trial and conviction of the man who was endangering the security of France. The facts of the case, however, revealed that the government did not have much to go on. A maid employed by the German Embassy in Paris and in the pay of the French counterintelligence service discovered a memorandum containing secret information about the French army written for the German military attaché, Colonel von Schwartzkoppen. French military intelligence immediately concluded that a French officer was in the pay of Germany, and that the officer must in some way be connected with the General Staff and familiar with its various operations. Such deductions limited the number of possible suspects; and, after a number of handwriting experts had compared the suspects' handwriting with that of the memorandum, the military officers concerned reached the hastily formed conclusion that the spy was a Captain Alfred Dreyfus, a native of Alsace. Their opinion was influenced by the fact that the man was a Jew. Dreyfus was summoned to Paris where, after having been tricked into taking dictation, he was accused of treason and given the opportunity to commit suicide, which he refused to do. The unfortunate captain was incarcerated in the Cherche-Midi prison until his court-martial.

The trial began on December 19, 1894. As Mâitre Demange, lawyer for the defense, hammered away at the evidence, the military authorities soon realized that they did not have a very good case. The Minister of War, General Mercier, and the intelligence officers were terrified of the effect that losing the case would have on public opinion, so they decided to bolster the case against Dreyfus by presenting a dossier made up for the most part of items that the judges considered to be incriminating. The defense was not permitted to see the dossier because it allegedly contained classified information. In the face of protests from Mâitre Demange that the court-martial was unfair, the judges convicted Dreyfus of treason. The captain was publicly stripped of his rank and insignia and sent to Devil's Island.

The painful campaign to clear Dreyfus of the charges was begun by his brother Mathieu who, with the help of Demange, soon discovered that the judges at the court-martial had been given evidence not made available to the defense. This constituted illegal procedure. The lawyer immediately demanded a retrial, which the army denied on the grounds that its honor and prestige as well as the security of the country depended upon defending the decision of December 1894 (*la chose jugée*). While Mathieu and his friends were working for a retrial, the new intelligence chief, Colonel Picquart, another Alsatian who had anti-Semitic leanings and no initial interest in seeing Dreyfus acquitted, was reviewing the evidence against the prisoner. What puzzled Picquart was the question of motive. He knew that military secrets were still being sold to Schwartzkoppen; and in 1896, another note written to the German military attaché fell into the hands of French intelligence. Its writer, a Commandant Esterhazy, scion of a great Hungarian family, had a poor reputation in Paris and was very much in debt. Colonel Picquart was immediately struck by the fact that the handwriting on this note was identical to that of the memorandum. The chief of intelligence went carefully over the dossier that had been presented to the judges at the court-martial and concluded that justice had not been done to Dreyfus. When he tried to persuade his superiors, including Chief of Staff Boisdeffre, that a retrial was necessary, they responded that it was in the interests of the army to respect *la chose jugée*. When Picquart continued to insist on a retrial, he was sent to Tunisia. The new chief of intelligence, Colonel Henry, had been privy to the secrets of the affair since 1894 and was convinced that military necessity required that Dreyfus be guilty.

By the end of 1896, the movement for revision of the verdict was under way. Picquart had informed the Parisian lawyer Labori of his findings, and soon the distinguished Alsatian Senator Scheurer-Kestner learned of Picquart's doubts. The Senator, who was a member of a well-known Republican family and related by marriage to Jules Ferry, had been in touch with the Dreyfus family, and he was dubious about the verdict. Scheurer-Kestner approached the President of the Republic, Félix Faure, and Premier Jules Méline, both of whom indicated that they preferred to respect the military's position on *la chose jugée*. On October 31, 1897, the newspaper *Le Matin* published the main outlines of Scheurer-Kestner's arguments in favor of revision; and on November 15, Mathieu Dreyfus, who had learned about Esterhazy, published a letter he had written to Minister of War Billot accusing Esterhazy of having written the memorandum. Such publicity was bound to excite public opinion, which had divided itself into Dreyfusard and anti-Dreyfusard factions.

The army was becoming concerned about the campaign that was being mounted in favor of revision, and Colonel Henry decided to strengthen its case by tampering with the evidence, not realizing that Picquart had photographed the Esterhazy note. Meanwhile Esterhazy, who knew that he had the support of the military, asked for a court-martial to clear him of Mathieu Dreyfus' charges. The court-martial took place on January 11, 1898. The military judges acquitted him in three minutes, much to the satisfaction of the crowd that was waiting outside the courtroom. A prince of the house of Orléans congratulated Esterhazy as he left the courtroom, and the anti-Dreyfusard press spoke of him as a possible Bonaparte.

The case for the revisionists seemed hopeless, but on January 13, 1897, Clemenceau's newspaper, *L'Aurore,* published a letter written by the distinguished novelist Émile Zola under the heading *J'accuse* charging the most important members of the military hierarchy with concealing evidence and accusing the military judges of deliberately acquitting the guilty Esterhazy. Immediately, Zola was arrested and brought to trial. On the witness stand Colonel Henry alluded mysteriously to secret dossiers affecting the nation's security. The novelist was found guilty, struck from the list of the Legion of Honor, and fined and sentenced to twelve months' imprisonment, which he ultimately escaped by fleeing to England, so often a refuge for Frenchmen in trouble.

A sense of frustration and despair hung heavy in the Dreyfusard camp. Neither the government, headed at the time of Zola's trial by Méline, nor the army would budge from the position that Dreyfus was fairly convicted; and popular opinion, if the anti-Semitic riots in Paris and Algiers are any indication, seemed to support this view. On July 7, 1898, the new Minister of War in the Brisson ministry, Godefroy Cavaignac, a member of a distinguished Republican family, made a speech in the Chamber referring to the massive evidence against Dreyfus. This speech so impressed the deputies that they voted overwhelmingly to have it posted on every official bulletin board in France.

Cavaignac was sincerely convinced of Dreyfus' guilt, and he believed that Colonel Picquart ought to be punished for his behavior. At the same time he indicated his disapproval of Esterhazy's conduct. In order to proceed against them both, he ordered a thorough review of the documents in the case. One of the officials in the intelligence office, looking at a letter particularly damaging to Dreyfus, realized that it was a forgery and immediately brought it to the attention of Cavaignac. Colonel Henry was summoned before the Minister of War and, under intensive questioning, admitted that he had tampered with the evidence to protect the army. The colonel was arrested and placed in prison where he committed suicide. On September 3, Cavaignac and the Chief of Staff Boisdeffre resigned. Both continued in their belief that, despite everything, Dreyfus was guilty.

The President of the Republic, Félixe Faure, was a staunch supporter of the army's position. This vain and rather pompous gentleman died suddenly on February 16, 1899, and he was replaced in his high office by Senator Émile Loubet by vote of the National Assembly which was now convinced that the anti-Dreyfusard campaign constituted a threat to the Republic. When Paul Déroulède and his revived League of Patriots tried to organize a *coup* on the occasion of President Faure's funeral, the threat to the Republic seemed even more real; and at this point, the Dreyfusard cause and the Republican cause became joined. On June 3, 1899, the Court of Criminal Appeal, which had decided to review the case, handed down the judgment that Dreyfus would have to be retried before a court-martial; and on June 9, 1899, the wretched captain boarded a vessel at Devil's Island to return to his hysterical homeland.

The second court-martial took place at the Breton city of Rennes in August 1899, while all the world watched to see if justice would be done. Despite all the evidence that now supported Dreyfus and despite the brilliant efforts of Demange and Labori in his behalf, the military judges could not bring themselves to impugn the honor of General Mercier and all the other officers who had maintained that Dreyfus was guilty. By a vote of five to two they found him guilty once again, but because of "extenuating circumstances" they sentenced him to ten years' imprisonment. The government headed by Waldeck-Rousseau immediately responded by appealing to President Loubet, who pardoned Dreyfus, bringing the affair to an end. In 1906, a civilian court of appeals annulled the verdict, and Dreyfus was reinstated in his old rank. He also received the Legion of Honor and was permitted to fight in World War I, proving to the world that the Republic was able to look after its own.

The impact of the Dreyfus affair was felt throughout France

and the world. Families were divided, and men who had been good friends never spoke to each other again. As the evidence in his favor mounted, Mark Twain and other foreigners were aghast that a nation such as France was being so obviously unfair to Dreyfus. Historians have not ceased to be fascinated by the affair, because the case was never solved satisfactorily and because explanations of its significance are so complex and have roots deep in the political and cultural soil of France.

The importance of the affair cannot be properly understood without understanding the impact of anti-Semitism at the end of the nineteenth century. "Scientific" sociological studies influenced by Comte and Darwin had emphasized the importance of race, and individuals like Maurice Barrès and Charles Maurras who sought to explain France's decline concluded that only when the nation was dominated again by the "French race" would it be restored to its rightful position as leader of Europe. Many Catholics believed that the Republic was controlled by Jews, Protestants, and Freemasons who by ruthlessly pressing the anticlerical campaign were destroying national traditions. The crash of the "Catholic" bank, the *Union générale,* appeared to them to be the result of a plot sponsored by the international Jewish syndicate. The fact that the Jews played an important role in French banking circles contributed to the development of anti-Semitic sentiments within the working class. This was exploited by men like Edouard Drumont who, in his popular book *La France Juive* (1886) and in his newspaper *La Libre Parole,* fulminated against the Jewish conquest of France. And the Christian Democratic movement begun in the 1890s also thrived on anti-Semitism. Hence the whole Dreyfus affair and the revisionist campaign appeared to be part of an enormous Jewish plot to those who wanted to believe that history is moved by conspiracy.

The Dreyfus affair was partly a product of the press, which was becoming more influential as a result of increased literacy and the cheaper cost of newspapers. French newspapers were notoriously partisan, a fact that does much to explain the political tensions that plagued the Republic throughout its existence. Anti-Dreyfusard papers, such as *L'Intransigeant, La Libre*

Parole, Le Figaro, and *La Croix,* as well as Dreyfusard newspapers, such as *L'Aurore* and *La Petite République,* made it difficult for Frenchmen to acquire an objective understanding of the issues involved.

The extraordinary role played by French intellectuals in the affair indicated the extent to which ideological values had come into conflict. Nationalists such as Jules Lemâitre, François Coppée, Ferdinand Brunetière, Maurice Barrès, and Paul Bourget, who became involved in the *Ligue de la Patrie Française* that was founded in 1898, reiterated the Machiavellian doctrine of *raison d'état* to justify the Dreyfus verdict. Charles Péguy, André Gide, Georges Sorel, and Marcel Proust saw in the affair a threat to the rights of man and argued that France would not survive if the ideals of the French Revolution were betrayed by the condemnation of an innocent man. These intellectuals formed the *Ligue pour la défense des droits de l'homme* to publicize the Dreyfusard position. In short, the revolutionary heritage and the anti-revolutionary heritage were very much involved in the quarrels of 1898 and 1899.

The affair was destined to remain a part of French political life from 1897 until the Liberation of France in 1945. The role of the Church and the army in the fight against revision revealed how alienated from the Republic these institutions had become. Young Monarchists and Bonapartists, unable to pursue political careers under the Republic, chose military and ecclesiastical careers, and they regarded the Revisionists' campaign as part of a plot to destroy sword and altar. The immediate political consequence of the affair, however, was to put a halt to the realignment of political forces around economic and social issues, and to focus attention once again on the constitutional question. This was a welcome relief to many who resisted this realignment. Intransigent Conservatives and Catholics were delighted to be able to point out how corrupt the Republic was and how unworthy of their adherence, an attitude which doomed the *Ralliement.* Opportunists such as Louis Barthou and Poincaré, who were dubious about Méline's conciliatory policy toward the Right, were able to use the affair as an excuse not to participate in a conservative

Republican party which would include anti-Dreyfusard *ralliés.* On the Left, Radicals afraid of cooperation with Socialists were pleased with the excuse to revive anticlericalism to avoid social reform; and although many Socialists followed Jaurès in defending the Republic against the anti-Dreyfusards, they preferred to regard the quarrel as derived from bourgeois interests. They believed that Socialist interests were best served by not getting involved in the controversy. The Dreyfus affair then became an excuse for reviving old political habits rather than adopting new ones.

4 / The Politics of
Radicalism, 1899–1914

THE SECOND ANTICLERICAL CAMPAIGN

In the spring of 1899, the Republic seemed to be in danger
from the tensions caused by the Dreyfus affair. The President of
the Republic, Émile Loubet, saw the need for a broadly based
ministry capable of resolving the crisis. After having tried unsuccessfully to enlist the services of Raymond Poincaré, he called
on René Waldeck-Rousseau, who accepted the task. Poincaré
had begun his political career as another one of Gambetta's lieutenants, and he had been responsible for the legislation of 1884
that legalized trade unions. Since then he had devoted most of
his time to becoming one of the nation's most effective lawyers.
The ministry formed by Waldeck-Rousseau was indeed broadly
based, including General de Gallifet from the Right as Minister
of War and the brilliant socialist lawyer Alexandre Millerand
from the Left as Minister of Commerce. Théophile Delcassé was
Minister of Foreign Affairs and Joseph Caillaux, eventually to
become the Radical leader, was Minister of Finance. Gallifet was
critical of the activity of some of his military colleagues during
the Dreyfus affair, but to many Radicals and Socialists he was
best known for his participation in the brutal suppression of the
Commune. When the Premier-designate presented his ministry
to the Chamber for confirmation on June 25, he was met with
cries of indignation from both the Right and the Left. The ministry received only the narrowest vote of confidence. It was

70

generally believed that the ministry would fall very soon. It lasted, however, until the elections of April 1902. The major problems confronting Waldeck-Rousseau were to quiet the furor over the Dreyfus affair and to establish the security of the regime against the supposed onslaughts of its enemies. From the Republican point of view, the main sources of trouble had been the army and the Church, both of which would have to be disciplined and brought into line. Gallifet kept a firm hand on the almost mutinous officer corps, and he issued an order to the army to the effect that the Dreyfus case was closed.

The Church presented special problems. Although the *Ralliement* had failed to secure the adherence of many Catholic priests and laymen to the Republic, Pope Leo XIII was still kindly disposed toward France. Waldeck-Rousseau, who had been raised in Catholic Brittany and had worked behind the scenes to make the *Ralliement* succeed, knew that another vicious anticlerical policy would only aggravate the tensions created by the Dreyfus affair. The government decided, therefore, to act against the most offensive Catholic elements; and in 1900, it ordered the dissolution of the Assumptionist order, whose influential newspaper *La Croix* had been almost as vitriolic as Drumont's *Libre Parole* in attacking the "Jewish" Republic. At the same time Waldeck-Rousseau tried to establish effective control over the religious orders that had never been covered in the Concordat of 1801 and were in the position of being semi-legal groups. In addition to this, the various orders owned considerable property that was to some extent tax-exempt (a situation reminiscent of the Old Regime), and the teaching orders were still deeply involved in the educational system despite the laical legislation of the 1880s. The Premier intended to enact laws that would give the government greater financial and political control over the regular clergy and reduce its educational influence. The parliamentary majority supporting the ministry, however, soon expressed the desire to go beyond Waldeck-Rousseau's plans, with the intention of eliminating rather than regulating the orders. The Law on Associations passed in July 1901 required all unauthorized orders to apply for authorization within three months (such authorization being granted in each particular case by the legislature) and forbade members of such orders to teach. The Premier, anxious to conciliate the Catholic community as much as possible, assured the Pope that any order seeking authorization would receive it; and Leo XIII, in turn, permitted the orders to seek recognition from the National Assembly.

The electoral campaign in the spring of 1902 centered around the religious question. (One priest saw it as a struggle between Barrabas and Jesus Christ.) Conservatives, *ralliés,* and Mélinists sought to protect the French Church, while other Opportunists, Radicals, and Socialists hoped for a mandate to step up anticlericalism. The number of votes in favor of the Left exceeded the number of votes supporting the Right by 200,000, but the *scrutin d'arrondissement,* which enabled prefects and schoolteachers to apply pressure at the local level, produced a new Chamber with a large majority determined to "defend the Republic." Waldeck-Rousseau resigned his office ostensibly for reasons of health, but the real reason was probably that he realized a conciliatory policy was now out of the question.

The new Premier, Émile Combes, epitomized the type of Radical politician who dominated France before World War I. As a young man, he had been a devout Catholic, and he began his career teaching theology in a secondary school in Normandy. But, after marrying into a bourgeois family, Combes renounced Catholicism and soon began to ascend the political ladder that led him from the mayor's office in Pons to the Senate and finally in the spring of 1902 to the Premier's office. *Petit père* Combes was an avid anticlerical, believing that his country would not enjoy the fruits of democracy until after Catholic influence was rooted out. Upon assuming office, he announced his intention of applying the Law on Associations rigorously, indicating that it would be extremely difficult for orders to receive authorization from the Chamber. In July 1902, the government closed 2500 girls' schools run by nuns; and, during the same year, charities and hospitals operated by unauthorized orders were shut down. One hundred and thirty-five orders were denied accreditation, while a few, primarily involved in missionary work, were permitted to continue their existence. Legislation was enacted in July 1904 that forbade even authorized orders the right to teach and required their complete suppression within ten years. Thousands of priests and nuns were forced into exile as a result of Combes' efforts. The property confiscated from the church went to private buyers instead of to charity as the government had originally promised.

The Combes ministry soon became involved in a quarrel with the Vatican over the centuries-old question of episcopal appointments. The Premier announced in 1902 that, contrary to the provisions of the Concordat of 1801, he would no longer seek the Pope's consent to the appointment of bishops. After the death of Leo XIII in 1904, he refused to appoint any bishop unless the Vatican cooperated. The new Pope, Pius X, was less conciliatory than his predecessor, and his Secretary of State, Merry del Val, an ardent Spanish royalist, appeared to be Rome's answer to the *petit père*. The conflict between the Catholic Church and the French government became even more acute when, in the spring of 1904, President Loubet paid a state visit to King Victor Emmanuel III in Rome, a visit that seemed to the Vatican to be French approval of Italian annexation of the Papal States. Pius X immediately sent a confidential circular to the various Catholic governments protesting Loubet's visit, but the Combes ministry did not want to break diplomatic relations with the Vatican at this point and decided to ignore the circular. When it was leaked to the socialist newspaper *L'Humanité* by the anticlerical Prince of Monaco, the government, anxious not to lose face, immediately recalled its ambassador to the Holy See. Meanwhile Pius X had summoned two French bishops to Rome to account for their excessively friendly attitude toward the Republic, but Combes refused to let them go. When the Vatican insisted, France broke diplomatic relations on July 30, 1904. In November, the ministry presented a proposal to the Chamber providing for separation of church and state.

The parliamentary majority that had supported Combes since 1902 was falling apart by 1905. The ministry was in deep trouble at the end of 1904, when it was interpellated in the

Chamber on the activities of the Minister of War. The Marquis de Gallifet had resigned from this office in June 1900 and was replaced by General André. In conformity with the government's efforts since 1899 to discipline Church and army, André had undertaken to "republicanize" the officer corps. He enlisted the cooperation of the Freemasons, who were fervently Republican, to ascertain which officers were worthy of promotion. Public utterances, the religious activities of one's wife, and children's education became the important factors in a successful military career. The disreputable activities of André and his associates were discovered in 1904, and the general was forced to resign. The Right continued its attacks on the ministry throughout the following year, when it was discovered that Combes was using André's methods to ensure the loyalty of the bureaucracy and the professoriat. Conservative antagonism, Socialist disillusionment with the government's poor record in the area of social legislation, and a general disgust with the anticlerical campaign even among Radicals like Clemenceau all combined to bring down the ministry in January 1905.

The new ministry, headed by Maurice Rouvier, approached the problem of separating church and state in a conciliatory manner. The law that was eventually passed on December 9, 1905, retained property that was used for religious purposes in the hands of the state but gave Catholics considerable control of it. This property would be on loan to local associations that were to be made up of priests and laymen, an arrangement approved by many French Catholics. Pius X, fearing schism and the threat to the ecclesiastical hierarchy, issued an encyclical, *Vehementer nos*, on February 11, 1906, condemning the entire arrangement. The Separation Law of 1906 called for an inventory of property used by the Church, and the government proceeded to execute the provision prior to lending the property to the associations, but the inventory takers set off riots in Catholic regions reminiscent of the disturbances brought about by the Civil Constitution of the Clergy in 1791. The government, now headed by Clemenceau, anxious to appease the Catholics and aware that the associations were prohibited because of Vatican disapproval, allowed the clergy to use the churches without the associations, thus bringing to an end the second anticlerical campaign within twenty-five years.

The French Catholic Church was in a deplorable condition at the time of separation. The elections of 1906, when the Right had lost 40 seats, were an indication of the fact that Conservatives had relatively little support. The process of de-Christianization that began in the eighteenth century reached a peak at the end of the nineteenth. The Church was poor in spirit and in resources. Recruitment of clergy was difficult because salaries were low and because the lack of religious vitality discouraged it. The Republic's effort to reduce Catholic influence on French education did have its effect, as evidenced in the dramatic increase in the number of civil marriages and non-baptized children after 1907.

However, separation produced important factors that would ultimately contribute to the revival of religious vitality in the country. The Church was for the first time in centuries free of political control. This meant that Catholicism was able to come to grips with the modern world on its own terms without fear of governmental interference. Catholic scholars began a careful reexamination of Catholic doctrine in order to discover what was suitable for the times, and young men like Marc Sangnier, through a group called *Le Sillon,* tried to commit Catholicism to the basic principles of social democracy. These "modernist" efforts failed initially because of conservative prejudices that dominated the Church, but they prepared the way for the ultimate reconciliation between the Catholic Church and the twentieth century. Certainly the freedom the French Church received in 1905 benefited the modernist movement.

THE *ACTION FRANÇAISE*

The second anticlerical campaign had serious political consequences. Intransigent Conservatives, *ralliés* such as Jacques Piou, and Opportunists who had followed Jules Méline and Eugène Spuller in the 1890s defended the Church and the Concordat against Republican attacks; but, in so doing, they permanently excluded themselves from governing circles. Bonapartists, Monarchists, and Catholics were poorly represented in the National Assembly and seemed doomed to political frustration. Some Monarchists retreated in disgust, resigning themselves to political impotence, but a significant element of the French Right that had become increasingly authoritarian and nationalistic since Boulanger began to proclaim the virtues of violence.

The *Action française* was the most important movement organized during the first decade of the twentieth century to appeal to the frustrated political instincts of the Right. Its founder, a young Provençal named Charles Maurras, had launched his literary career in defense of Colonel Henry; and, after the close of the affair in 1899, he sought to sustain the anti-Republican vigor of Déroulède's *Ligue des Patriotes*, the *Ligue de la Patrie française*, and *La Croix*, which were threatened with extinction by the revisionist victory. In July 1899, Maurras launched the fortnightly *Revue de l'Action Française*, which became a daily in 1908 with the help of Léon Daudet, son of the novelist Alphonse Daudet. In 1905, the *Ligue d'Action Française* was organized and, in 1906, the *Institut d'Action Française*—both for the purpose of expounding Maurras' ideas. The *Camelots du roi* was organized in 1908 by youthful *maurrasiens* who hawked the newspaper in the streets and carried out strong-arm tactics whenever the occasion arose.

Maurras, much influenced by Auguste Comte, believed that a scientific study of French history showed that only a monarchy was capable of maintaining French unity and restoring the nation to its preeminent position among the nations of Europe. France had to be true to its traditions and its race, which meant destroying the Republic and ridding society of such corrupting elements as Jews and Protestants. Like many Conservatives who detested the "political games" that passed for political action in the Chamber, Maurras had no illusions about bringing a royal restoration by parliamentary procedure. The violent overthrow of the corrupt regime would reflect the "absolute will to win" necessary to make France a great nation once again.

Many Monarchists and Catholics, including the Duc d'Orléans, were attracted to the *Action française*, despite the sensibilities of older Orléanists devoted to the principles of constitutional monarchy and despite the misgivings of the Vatican about the movement's emphasis on the political rather than the spiritual mission of the Church. The movement appealed to certain elements within French Catholicism who deplored their loss of political power after the separation of church and state. The *Action française* drew much of its support, however, from lawyers, clerical workers, shopkeepers, teachers, traveling salesmen, and other groups within the lower middle class who were drawn to the patriotic message and the attacks on the regime that they held responsible for their economic difficulties. Many students in the universities, particularly the Sorbonne, were aware of the Republic's inability to provide dynamic leadership, and they were naturally attracted to a movement that stressed action. To some extent, the *Action française* made up for the lack of Rightist political influence; and although the movement was relatively small before 1914, it did contribute to the revival of the Right and kept the anti-Republican flame alive after the Dreyfus affair.

THE LEFT

The parliamentary majority that supported the Waldeck-Rousseau and Combes ministries between 1899 and 1905 was made up of a number of groups. Waldeck-Rousseau, Louis Barthou, and Raymond Poincaré were former Opportunists who had broken with Méline on the question of the *Ralliement*. The Socialists reluctantly associated themselves with the majority because of Jaurès' firm conviction that their cause was best served by defending the Republic. The most powerful element within the majority consisted of the Radicals, who were to dominate the Third Republic from the Dreyfus era to the fall of France in 1940. The major political question during the period between 1899 and 1909 was whether it was possible to construct a homogeneous party on the Left, just as the major political issue between 1890 and 1898 had been whether a homogeneous party could be formed on the Right.

When Émile Combes became Premier in 1902, he took steps

to develop a disciplined majority by organizing a steering committee of representatives from each of the groups supporting the
ministry (*Délégation des gauches*). This committee was charged
with the responsibility of getting favorable votes for the government in the Chamber and in the Senate. Deputies were told that
their political careers might be ended if they did not support
the government. At the same time, Combes sought to maintain
discipline at the grass roots level by organizing local electoral
committees to keep an eye on the deputies and to instruct departmental prefects in the use of the patronage system as a means
of securing loyalty. The Premier soon discovered, however, that
a homogeneous party could be established only if there was
general agreement on basic political issues. The issue that
Combes hoped would sustain his majority was, of course, anticlericalism, but it was not enough to cover up the fundamental
differences of opinion on economic and social matters that separated the various groups. Also, many Republicans and Socialists
were disgusted by the anticlerical campaign that was producing
such bitterness in France.

Since the 1890s, the Radicals had been plagued by the "social question." Some, including Ferdinand Buisson, urged the
party to resolve the problems of an industrial society by sponsor-
ing social legislation and by maintaining cordial relations with the
Socialists. "It is a contradiction," he wrote in 1906, "that the
people should be at once sovereign and downtrodden." Other
Radicals, the majority, agreed with Clemenceau that France
should maintain the sanctity of private property in the face of
Socialist demands. They were the provincial lawyers, doctors,
and shopkeepers who believed that the aims and aspirations of
the French Revolution had been achieved and that the nation
under the Third Republic was safely in the hands of the *petit
propriétaire*. Most Radicals reflected the conservative interests of
rural France, and they were unsympathetic to the Socialist demands for legislation to improve the condition of the urban
worker since the Socialists represented groups and interests which
were to them threatening French traditions. The political strength
of the Radicals was twofold: they did represent the interests of

the majority of Frenchmen, and they were able to adjust policy to local conditions. The Radicals were weak as a national party but strong at the grass-roots level; and, in a country where local issues were dominant, this proved to be an advantage.

At the turn of the century, the Socialists were faced with the problem of either accepting Radical leadership or rejecting it in favor of Marxist principles that were geared to industrialization and urbanization. A leading Socialist, Millerand, had accepted a ministerial portfolio in 1899, and Jaurès cooperated with the *Délégation des gauches* from 1902 to 1905. But Millerand's action increased the tensions that already existed within the Socialist movement. Jaurès defended Millerand's participation in the Waldeck-Rousseau ministry as a first step in the eventual Socialist mastery of the Republic, hoping that more social legislation might be enacted to improve the condition of the proletariat. Jaurés believed that Millerand's portfolio was an excellent indication of how far the Socialists had come since the Commune. Guesde, on the other hand, argued that Millerand's action, if encouraged, would destroy the movement because it negated the Marxist principle of Socialist Party opposition to bourgeois regimes. From Guesde's point of view, the *cas Millerand* revealed a crass, opportunistic streak in French Socialism that would lead to its *embourgeoisement* by the Republic.

On December 3, 1899, representatives of the various Socialist groups met in Paris to debate the issue of "ministerialism"; and, after much discussion, an equivocal resolution was passed condemning Socialist participation in the ministry on principle, but recognizing "certain exceptional circumstances" that might make such participation necessary. No one was satisfied by the resolution, and the Millerand case continued to plague French and European socialism.

The leading figures of the European Socialist movement convened in Amsterdam in August 1904 to resolve once and for all whether the Socialist movement in general should strive for the alleviation of workers' conditions within the existing social and legal framework, or whether it should remain in perpetual opposition to bourgeois institutions. After impassioned speeches, by Jaurès and Guesde among others, the congress adopted a resolution stating that "social democracy could accept no participation in the government within the capitalist system." This meant that the advocates of perpetual opposition had won. The congress also called for the formation of unified Socialist parties in each country. Pursuant to this end, French Socialists met in Paris in April 1905 and announced that henceforth they were members of a party that would call itself the *Parti socialiste, section française de l'internationale ouvrière* or Socialist Party, French Section of the Workers' International (SFIO). The fundamental principles of the party were Marxist-oriented and included (1) an international understanding among all workers, (2) the organization of the working class in order to capture political power, and (3) the socialization of the means of production and exchange.

French socialism rejected the arguments of Jaurès and Millerand in favor of cooperation with bourgeois parties and ministries wherever possible. This meant that future participation within the *Délégation des gauches* was out of the question. Jaurès accepted the decision at Amsterdam, but a number of young Socialist deputies—including Millerand, Aristide Briand, and René Viviani, all future stalwarts of the Republic—abandoned the movement in order to pursue ministerial careers.

There were a number of reasons for the repudiation of the "ministerialists" within the Socialist movement. The Radicals were not very interested in social legislation. Millerand as a minister had seen to it that existing factory legislation was enforced, that the ten-hour day became mandatory for all workers. He had also worked for the establishment of a Ministry of Labor, which came into being in 1906. A great deal more legislation of this sort, including provisions for old-age pensions, was needed, however, and the Radicals were dragging their feet. Socialists regarded themselves as the representatives of labor, but the French trade unions were clearly suspicious of Socialists who advocated cooperation with the bourgeois regime; and during the period when Socialism was associated with the *Délégation des gauches,* the unions preferred to act on their own. The formation of the unified Socialist Party, which put class ahead of country, paved the way for closer cooperation between the party and the unions. By pitting itself against the regime, the Socialist Party attracted other discontented elements, including lower echelon civil servants whose wages lagged behind rising prices.

Differences of opinion on a number of issues continued to plague the Socialists even though they had organized a unified party in 1905. There were those who continued to hope for greater cooperation between the SFIO and other parties on the Left, while others argued that the State, instead of being an instrument of oppression, was the means for achieving a Socialist society. Socialists defended strikes in the Chamber, but many, including Guesde, remained suspicious of the syndicalist impulse within the trade union movement because it seemed undisciplined. After 1905, as the international situation worsened, Socialists debated the question of what to do in the event of war. Should they work for peace even to the extent of cooperating with other parties? Should they attempt to prevent war by encouraging a general strike? Or should Socialists stand aside and let the bourgeois states tear themselves apart? Marx had proclaimed that the worker had no country and that his loyalty belonged to his class. This thesis was extremely difficult for French workers or Socialist politicians to accept because they were patriotic and because the great revolutionary tradition embodied the ideal that France must be defended against her enemies. Jaurès regarded himself as a patriot, but he did not believe that a European war would serve the interests of the working class or his country. The compelling nature of some of these problems between 1905 and 1914 accentuated these differences of opinion and prevented the SFIO from acting resolutely or effectively.

The *Délégation des gauches* fell apart in 1905, primarily because its two most important groups faced in different directions. The Radicals clung to the traditions of rural France, while the Socialists, although making concessions to the poorer peasants, looked ahead to an industrial and urban France. The Radicals eschewed disciplined central-party control for flexibility at the local level, while the Socialists attempted to form a disciplined, unified party dedicated to general principles. The elections of 1906 revealed that the Radicals had considerable political support throughout the country. They claimed 250 out of the 420 deputies from the various groups that made up the *Délégation des gauches*. They could count on the support of the independent Socialists who were inclined to support the government; and, on questions relating to economic liberalism and social order, they could count on the support of the Right. A clear indication of Radical strength in the Chamber was the fact that Georges Clemenceau was named Premier for the first time in November 1906 and that he remained in office until July 1909.

Clemenceau typified the evolution of Radicalism toward the Right. In 1881, he had announced a program calling for social legislation, hoping to appeal to the urban worker as well as the peasant. Since that time, the Socialists had secured the support of the proletariat, and Clemenceau and his followers learned that there were indeed "enemies to the Left" claiming that the Revolution had not run its course. The new Premier, in his many debates with Jaurès during his term of office, pitted the free development of the individual and the sanctity of private property against collectivism. During this time, he had ample opportunity to make known his social policy.

Between 1906 and 1911, France was plagued with strikes by railroad workers, longshoremen, miners, and others. Although the country was in the process of recovering from the recession, the recovery was uneven. The purchasing power of the lower classes was weakened by the fact that wages still lagged badly behind prices. Another reason for the strikes was the attitude of employers toward trade unions and collective bargaining, which from their point of view violated the principles of economic liberalism. The *patrons* made it difficult for unions to recruit workers in their factories, and they hired "scab" labor and encouraged "yellow dog" contracts as a means of protecting themselves against strikes, which in turn encouraged syndicalist sentiment in the unions. At the same time, the union movement began to attract civil servants and schoolteachers, who were also affected by low wages. Postal workers and other lower echelon *fonctionnaires* hoped to unionize in order to put pressure on the government by threatening to disrupt public services, thereby drawing the attention of the electorate to their plight.

Clemenceau, who called himself "France's number one cop," did not hesitate to use force to protect the interests of the employers and the scab labor. In 1907, he turned the army on the peasants in the Midi who were demonstrating and rioting because of the sharp drop in the price of wine. Nor would the Premier permit the civil servants or schoolteachers to unionize, arguing that such action constituted a threat to public order. The ministry—which included two former Socialists, Briand and Viviani—made little effort to enact legislation to improve the condition of the laboring poor. Much to the horror of conservative sentiment, the government did take over one private railroad which was running up a large deficit, but the former owners made a great profit out of the transaction.

Jaurès, the major spokesman for the SFIO, steadfastly attacked Radical hypocrisy in the Chamber. What was particularly galling to the Socialists was the policy of Aristide Briand, formerly an advocate of syndicalism, who had abandoned the movement and become Premier in 1910. In October, a strike broke out against the Northern Railroad Company, where workers whose wages over a thirty year period had hardly risen at all were demanding higher salaries and strict enforcement of the six-day week. The company, whose profits had been climbing steadily because of the general economic recovery since 1900, refused even to discuss the union's demands, preferring instead to eliminate overtime without making arrangements for a compensatory wage increase. The strike involved worker violence in retaliation for the company's dismissal of some of the labor leaders, and it had a detrimental effect on one of the nation's most important industrial regions. The government and many of the leading newspapers were unsympathetic to the workers, arguing that a strike of railwaymen was a crime because it was against the public interest to tie up communications and disrupt national defense. When violence broke out, Briand immediately issued a decree conscripting the employees of the five main railroad companies into the army for twenty-one days, thus ending the strike. The uncompromising attitude of Clemenceau and Briand on social questions made it obvious that the gap between the Radicals and the Socialists was widening, that the possibility of developing a political party on the Left that would be dedicated to the cause of social democracy appeared to be remote.

THE NATIONALIST REVIVAL

French nationalism was a product of the Revolution of 1789 and as such was associated with the Left until the Boulanger crisis. The Paris Commune was partly the result of frustrated Jacobinism, whereas the elections of 1871 revealed the pacifist, anti-nationalist sentiments of the Right. By 1914, the tables were turned. The Left tended toward pacifism, whereas the Right was aggressively nationalist. Monarchists and Bonapartists dominated the officer corps, and they suffered particularly because of the humiliation of 1871. The French army, with the help of the Church's missionary efforts, did much toward constructing an empire in Africa and Asia. It was in the sands of Tunisia and in the jungles of Indo-China that the officer corps recovered its pride after the humiliation of 1871. The Right was as proud of the army as it was disgusted with the Republic, a fact which was reflected in Conservative support of Boulanger and defense of military honor at the time of the Dreyfus affair. By 1900, patriotism had become synonymous with anti-Republicanism. The regime had let the nation down, and it was this conviction that Maurras exploited. According to the *Action française*, the army and the Church were essentially French, while the Republic was Semitic, Protestant, and alien to French culture.

Between 1881 and 1905, the Republican leaders were generally content to accept German supremacy on the continent and to concentrate primarily on domestic issues and on constructing defensive alliances against German expansion. From 1905 to 1914, the international situation worsened. Kaiser Wilhelm II's saber-rattling speech in Morocco and the growing instability in the Balkans caused many politicians to conclude that war was inevitable. The nationalist revival after 1905 came about because many Frenchmen believed that there ought to be a greater sense of national purpose. During those years, the Joan of Arc cult, which appealed to Republicans and Conservatives alike, symbolized a quest for national identity. But nationalism also appealed to those who, in the name of law and order, resisted the growing demand for social legislation. Radicals, no longer able to use the anticlerical issue to divert attention from social and economic problems, now used the "national interest" as an excuse to resist pressures from the Left. The nationalist revival, like the *Ralliement,* provided an opportunity for conservative forces to regroup to defend their interests and their country.

Raymond Poincaré was the man who, more than anyone else, epitomized the nationalist revival among Republicans. Born in Lorraine and educated as a lawyer, he had entered politics in the 1890s as an Opportunist, but he split with Méline in 1898 and eventually joined the Dreyfusards in defending the Republic. Poincaré was intensely conservative on economic and social questions, believing that the working class should resolve its problems through thrift and hard work rather than through legislation. In a speech delivered in 1895, Poincaré appealed to patriotism as the only means of unifying Frenchmen. He was not a warmonger, but as international tensions increased—particularly after Germany precipitated the second Moroccan crisis by sending a gunboat to Agadir in 1911—Poincaré concluded that war was inevitable and that the country had better be prepared.

In January 1912, as a wave of patriotic sentiment swept over the country in the wake of the Moroccan crisis, Poincaré was appointed Premier. In 1913, with war clouds gathering on the horizon, the typically mediocre President Armand Fallières completed his term of office, and nationalists of every shade and description supported Poincaré as candidate for that office. He was opposed by a virtually unknown Radical who, under normal circumstances given Republican prejudice against strong men, would have won the election. But, because of strong nationalist sentiment and the desire for strong leadership in time of crisis, Poincarè was elected on the second ballot.

In 1913, nationalist sentiment reached a peak in the quarrel over the "Three-Year Law." Universal military service had been in effect in France since the war with Prussia, but Republicans, loyal to the revolutionary concept of a citizen army, had traditionally supported as short a term of military service as possible. In the wake of the Dreyfus affair, the term of service for every male citizen was cut from three years to two. As the international situation became worse, the army became concerned about its size in comparison with the size of the German army. In 1912, in response to the Balkan crisis, Germany undertook a vast program of rearmament. Because of this, the French government decided that it would be necessary to reinstitute the three-year requirement. In July 1913, in the face of violent opposition from those opposed to the nationalist revival, the Three-Year Law was passed in the Chamber (by a vote of 339 to 223); and shortly thereafter, it was passed by the Senate.

THE INCOME TAX AND THE ELECTION OF 1914

Resurgent nationalism, which had brought about a rapprochement between the various conservative forces also forced, in opposition, a rapprochement between political forces on the Left. Most Socialists were convinced that nationalism was an excuse to divert attention from social problems, and they believed with Jaurès that a European war could only serve the interests of imperialism and the armament industry and not the proletariat. Radicals were divided over the nationalist revival. Many supported Poincaré, while others became alarmed because the revival violated a number of Republican traditions, including the weak presidency and the two-year military service. Some Radicals distrusted the big bankers and industrialists, whom they felt were exploiting the international situation to their own advantage. They were also well aware of pacifist sentiments at the local level.

The man who, with Jaurès, headed the resistance to the nationalist revival was Joseph Caillaux, whose father had been Finance Minister under the Duc de Broglie in 1877. Brought up in Orléanist circles, Caillaux was elected to the Chamber as a Republican in 1898. Because of his connections with banking circles and because of his experience as a financial administrator, the young deputy was named Minister of Finance by Waldeck-Rousseau in 1899, a move which caused jealousy among older Republicans who had been passed over. Caillaux was conservative on many issues, but he was appalled by the inefficient and ineffective tax structure of the country. France had not progressed very far in tax reform since the Revolution. In fact, the tax problems at the end of the nineteenth century were similar to what they had been a hundred years earlier. There were numerous indirect taxes that hampered commerce and industry; and the burden of direct taxation was still on land rather than on industry, which was now producing much of the nation's wealth. Caillaux proposed tax reforms similar to those advanced by the physiocrats, calling for a simplified tax system to include a tax on all incomes.

The progressive income tax had been a major bone of contention between the Left and the Right since the Republic was founded. The Left argued that it provided for a fairer distribution of the tax burden, while conservatives argued that such a tax was a violation of property rights. As an issue, the income tax was particularly significant because it was one of the few pieces of social legislation on which Radicals and Socialists could agree and because, along with the nationalist revival, it helped to bring about a new realignment of political forces. On June 26, 1911, Caillaux became Premier; and, although he made it clear that he would deal firmly with strikers, he announced his intention to introduce the income tax. The Premier was chiefly interested in domestic problems, but it was during his ministry that the second Moroccan crisis reached its peak, and he was forced to concern himself with foreign affairs as well. Caillaux resolved the crisis by giving Germany territory in Africa in return for a free hand in Morocco. The policy of the

Caillaux ministry—which fell early in 1912 to be succeeded by Poincaré's first ministry—contributed substantially to the political realignment that was taking place on the eve of the war.

The elections of May 1914 were fought on the issues of the Three-Year Law and the income tax. The importance of these issues was such that, on the second ballot, the Socialists temporarily abandoned their policy of not cooperating with the Radicals. Feelings ran high during the electoral campaign; and the editor of the conservative *Le Figaro,* Gaston Calmette, went to great lengths to discredit Caillaux, even to the extent of publishing letters that had been written to Caillaux by his wife when she was his mistress. This so enraged Madame Caillaux that she forced her way into Calmette's office and shot him to death, causing a great scandal. The elections ended in a great victory for the Left—particularly the Socialists—who again, as in 1893, profited from Republican scandals. The Socialists won 1,400,000 votes and 103 seats in the Chamber, thereby becoming the second largest party. The Radicals, led by Caillaux, won 136 seats.

Exercising his presidential prerogative and hoping to protect the Three-Year Law, Poincaré refused to call on Caillaux to form a government. A former Socialist, René Viviani, became Premier in June; and, in the following month, both chambers passed the income tax, although it did not go into effect until a later period. At the end of June, when the Archduke Ferdinand was shot at Sarajevo, the Three-Year Law was no longer an issue. The nation was being readied for war. Jean Jaurès exerted every effort to persuade Socialists of all countries to prevent war by a general strike, but even French Socialists found it difficult to put class ahead of country when confronted with the German juggernaught. On July 31, Jaurès, who had tried to persuade his countrymen that the humanitarian and cosmopolitan ideals of the Enlightenment were worth far more than the nationalist ideal of the Revolution, was assassinated; and on August 3, France went to war. Viviani was able to reconstruct his cabinet to include the monarchist Denys Cochin and the Marxist Jules Guesde, in the name of "sacred union," a union which scarcely covered up the division that had troubled the country as recently as the May elections.

The political history of France between 1899 and 1914 began with Republicans and Socialists defending the regime against its enemies, the army and the Church. In 1905 as in 1890, politics shifted away from Republican defense to the pressing economic and social questions that needed to be resolved. Royalist and Republican conservatives, in spite of the Dreyfus affair and the clerical issue, were able to find common ground during the nationalist revival. (Even the *Action française* was pleased by the election of Poincaré to the presidency in 1913.) By 1914, a conservative party, based not upon constitutional questions but upon economic issues, was in the making.

The realignment of political forces on the Left is more difficult to assess. Radicals and Socialists were at sword's point in 1910 because they were unable to agree on social policy. In 1914, however, both groups were able to unite on common ground. The nationalist revival and the income tax contributed to this. The decline of syndicalism within the trade union movement after 1910 and the willingness of labor leaders to work within the legal framework strengthened the impulse within the SFIO to cooperate with other parties. The Radicals were clearly not interested in too much social reform, and the Socialists would have been forced to compromise their revolutionary principles to a considerable extent in order to cooperate with the more conservative group. Given the evident willingness of many Socialists to work within the Republican system and given the conservative nature of French society and institutions, the Socialists would very likely have made the necessary compromises and adjustments. The war and the Russian Revolution intervened, however, and again altered the political alignments on the Left.

5 / France's Role in World Affairs, 1870-1914

FRENCH IMPERIAL EXPANSION

In 1870, France was forced to relinquish her dominant position in Europe, a position she had maintained since the seventeenth century, which helps to explain the sense of frustration that produced the Boulanger crisis and the Dreyfus affair. The German Empire, which had been the battleground of foreign armies for centuries, was now the most powerful state on the continent. And a large part of the diplomatic history of Europe between 1871 and 1914 is involved with the attempts of the major powers to adjust to this shift. Yet France's role in European and world affairs remained considerable, one of the principal reasons being that, by 1900, she had acquired a world-wide empire in Africa second only to that of Great Britain. During the seventeenth century, French explorers, merchants, and colonists had built an empire in the Western Hemisphere and in India rivaling Britain's; but Louis XIV and his successor, having to choose between continental and imperial interests, chose the former. By 1789, the French empire was reduced to a few islands in the West Indies and in the St. Lawrence River, with a few trading posts in West Africa and India. During the course of the nineteenth century, France gradually and quite haphazardly constructed a second empire despite the fact that her primary concern continued to be Europe.

In 1830, Charles X, eager for international prestige, sent a military expedition to Algeria, and so began the French conquest of North Africa. France had been a Mediterranean power since the sixteenth century; and, when the Ottoman Empire's hold on the Mahgreb weakened and French commercial interests were threatened by pirates and by warring tribes, it became necessary for the French army to intervene. All of Algeria was conquered by 1870, but her future relationship with the mother country had yet to be determined. The new "colony" differed from other French colonies in that it contained a large number of French settlers, political refugees, and adventurous entrepreneurs. Since the natives were incapable of holding on to it, these *colons* grabbed up most of the fertile land and succeeded in developing large estates that produced wheat and wine. Other Frenchmen established lucrative businesses in the modern cities of Algiers, Constantine, and Oran. The Arab population, several times larger than the European, had to be content either with inferior positions in the European sectors or with nomadic life in the desert.

The French controlled the politics and economy of Algeria entirely. The country was attached to metropolitan France, divided into departments, and administered by the Ministry of the Interior in the same way as other French departments. Algeria was represented in both the Senate and the Chamber of Deputies, but only Arabs who had renounced Moslem law and polygamy were eligible to become representatives of their country. In 1896, the position of Governor-General was revived because the government in Paris realized that Algerian problems were substantially different from those of the metropole; but, even though efforts were made to treat the Arab population more justly, the major distinctions between the European community and the Islamic community were maintained.

Tunisia was nominally part of the Ottoman Empire, and the Bey of Tunis was ostensibly the Sultan's regent in that principality. The regency of Tunisia in the 1870s was in a chaotic condition. Warring tribes caused political unrest, and the luxurious tastes of the Bey had created a large national debt, most of which was owed to various European enterprises exploiting the region. Italian, French, and British businessmen became deeply involved in Tunisian affairs; and, as the Bey's indebtedness and political instability increased, it was only a matter of time before one or more European powers would intervene. Italy and France were the two most interested powers. Italy's interest was because of a large number of her citizens living in Tunisia and because control of both Tunis and Sicily would make her a major Mediterranean power. France's interest arose from the proximity of the Regency to Algeria and from her numerous business enterprises there. The French government managed to gain the support of England and Germany; and, when a number of incidents occurred on the Algerian frontier, the French army used them as an excuse to invade and occupy Tunisia. Italy protested vainly, but she was ultimately forced to accept French hegemony in the region. By the Treaty of Bardo drawn up in 1881, Tunisia became a protectorate of France. From this, France came to control the domestic and foreign affairs of the country even though the form of government remained the same. Unlike the nomadic Algerians, the Tunisians were fairly sophisticated, politically as well as economically, which meant that they participated to a greater extent in the modernization of their country than the Algerians did in theirs.

When Egypt loosened its ties with the Ottoman Empire, France's traditional involvement in Mediterranean and North African affairs caused her to take an interest in that ancient kingdom. Napoleon and Louis Philippe both tried to exercise some kind of control over Egypt, and it was Ferdinand de Lesseps —a Frenchman—who built the Suez Canal to be owned and operated by a company composed mainly of French shareholders. England, as the largest single shareholder in the Suez Canal Company, was also interested in Egypt because 80 percent of the shipping that passed through the canal was British.

The political situation of Egypt in mid-century was much the same as that of Tunisia. Turkey exercised a nominal suzerainty over the country, but the viceroy (Khedive) was virtually autonomous. The Khedive Ismail was anxious to modernize his country and built railroads, opera houses, and palaces that were financed by British and French enterprises. The British and French governments became deeply involved in Egyptian affairs when the Khedive showed himself to be incapable of fiscal responsibility, but intervention by the European powers stimulated Egyptian nationalism, causing uprisings in 1881 throughout the country. France and England agreed that military intervention was necessary, but France hesitated to join England in occupying Egypt because of a domestic political crisis. England proceeded to establish her own protectorate over Egypt, much to the annoyance of the French who exerted considerable but belated pressure to get the British out of the area. Only when the Entente Cordiale was drawn up during 1903 and 1904 did France finally acquiesce to British control of Egypt.

France completed her conquest of North Africa by establishing a protectorate over Morocco in 1911. The Moroccan Empire was independent at the turn of the century; but, like so many other North African principalities, it was also on the verge of anarchy because the Sultan was unable to exercise control over rebellious tribes. Like Tunisia and Egypt, Morocco was being exploited by foreign interests, and the Sultan's government was practically bankrupt. France was especially anxious to gain control over the country because it would establish a link between her North African holdings and her Central African territories and because Morocco was strategically located at the entrance to the Mediterranean. In 1902, the French government began to draw up plans to "pacify" the North African empire. France did acquire British support, but she met resistance from Spain and Germany.

At the Algeciras Conference in 1905, France and Spain were jointly given the right to intervene in Morocco, but the fruits of economic exploitation were to be made available to all interested powers. Continued political unrest in the region, as well as continued pressure from the French army at the Algerian border, required a revision of the Algeciras accords; and in 1911, a Franco-German agreement provided France with a free hand in Morocco. Spain would receive a strip of territory opposite Gibraltar to compensate for the establishment of a

French protectorate over the larger part of the empire. Moroccan institutions were retained, but as with Tunisia, France maintained a controlling voice in the affairs of the country. In 1914, the main problem confronting the French in Morocco was pacification, particularly in the mountain regions where rebellious tribes still refused to submit to central authority.

Since the seventeenth century, France had maintained commercial ties with Senegal, once a major slave-trading center. During the latter half of the nineteenth century, French exploratory expeditions used it as a base for establishing trading posts on the Ivory Coast and in Guinea. In 1875, a young French naval officer, Pierre de Brazza-Savorgnan, began to explore the Congo basin to insure that French presence in the area was maintained in the face of the Congo Free State organized by the Belgian King Leopold II. The European powers, including England, who were interested in exploiting Central Africa sent representatives to the Berlin Conference of 1885 where they reached an agreement on the method for marking out colonies and exploiting the resources of the dark continent. In order to claim a colony in Central Africa, a power was obliged to establish an effective presence there after having notified the other powers of its intention.

After the Berlin Conference, the scramble for African colonies began in earnest. France's primary interest was to push east from her bases on the West African coast in hopes of cutting the British off from the upper Nile and connecting (by way of Ethiopia where the French government was hoping to acquire influence) with her small colony of Somaliland. Fear of war with Great Britain in 1899 prevented the French from realizing these dreams, but the country nevertheless had taken control of valuable territory in Central Africa. Her holdings south of the Sahara produced a number of commodities for the world market including cocoa, palm oil, timber, rubber, and cotton. The construction of a railroad system was essential for effective economic exploitation of the region, but this was not accomplished until after World War I. The main problem confronting the French in Central and West Africa was to administer areas where native political institutions were primitive and incapable of adaptation to modern use. A Ministry of Colonies was created in France in 1894 to determine policy; and, in the same year, a colonial council was formed to represent white interests in colonies throughout the world. Schools were set up that would enable ambitious natives to obtain the benefits of French civilization, and educated Africans were eligible for minor administrative positions. However, little effort was made to encourage native culture, which was regarded as inferior.

The island of Madagascar became part of the French Empire in 1896. The French had been interested in it since the reign of Louis XIV; but since the Napoleonic era, the major influence in Madagascar was British. As a result of ties with tribes that were at odds with the native king, France regained a foothold on the island. She signed a treaty in 1885 giving her control over the strategic harbor of Diego-Suarez. Judicious tribal alliances along with military action enabled France to annex Madagascar in 1896. Despite friction among the various tribes and despite native customs that made modernization difficult, every effort was made to administer the new colony through native institutions. The French originally intended the island to be a producer of tropical crops, but conditions were inappropriate, and it became used chiefly for raising cattle.

French interest in Southeast Asia also dates to the reign of Louis XIV, when efforts had been made to establish ties with Siam. During the reign of Louis XVI, the Emperor of Annam sent an ambassador to Versailles. Since that time, missionaries and adventurers had become deeply involved in Indo-China. This region consisted of a number of kingdoms that included the Empire of Annam, which was a feudatory of China and whose ties with China were strong culturally but weak politically. Within Annam was the territory of Tonkin with easily accessible trade routes by sea and by the Red River to China. The Tonkinese resented the rule of the Annamites, and friction between the two peoples provided opportunities for foreign intervention. South of Annam lay Cochin-China, which had a rather meager population. But Cochin-China also contained the Mekong Delta, which had great agricultural potential. West of Annam and bordering on Siam were situated the kingdoms of Cambodia and Laos, whose cultural ties were with Indic civilization and whose political institutions were weak.

During the Second Empire, the French had pushed into Chochin-China, where they established a colony in 1870. Taking advantage of unrest and persecution of Christian minorities by the Annamites, a French military expedition moved into Tonkin. They also took full advantage of the commercial possibilities; and in 1873, an expedition led by a young naval officer seized Hanoi, the capital of Tonkin. In 1874, by the Treaty of Hué, the Annamese government allowed the French to establish a protectorate over Tonkin; but, as the French continued to expand in the area, the Annamese appealed to China for protection. In 1883, France was faced with fighting the second Tonkinese War against Annam and China. The French government, headed by Jules Ferry, was in an awkward position. Public opinion did not want a war with China because of the expense and because a war in a far-off place would weaken French defense capabilities at home. French operations in Annam had to be limited. Even so, the meager French forces were able to subjugate Annam; and, by the Treaty of Tientsin in 1884, France established another protectorate over the whole empire. China refused to accept the provisions of the treaty, and the war continued, with a French expeditionary force occupying Formosa briefly, while a French naval squadron destroyed a Chinese fleet. Ferry hoped for a crushing victory over China before public opinion knew what was happening, but French forces suffered a defeat on the Chinese border, and the discredited Ferry ministry fell. In April 1885, France and China came to terms; and by the second Treaty of Tientsin, China renounced her suzerainty over Annam and evacuated Hanoi, opening the doors for France. France also established a protectorate over Cambodia in 1885, and over Laos, in 1893, despite protests from Siam and Britain. In 1899, as a result of the "partition" of China, France acquired extensive commercial rights in the Chinese territory adjacent to Tonkin.

French administration of her Indo-Chinese empire varied according to the particular kingdom or region. Some effort was made to preserve political, social, and cultural institutions, but often important bureaucratic positions were given to incompetent Frenchmen with little administrative experience, a practice which caused resentment. One major problem was pacifying areas of the country that were plagued by bandits who had been encouraged by China. Another was subduing villages that refused to accept the authority imposed on them by Saigon or Hanoi. One method of restoring order was the "splash of oil" system, by which a village that had been pacified became a market center and was given arms to defend itself against bandits. A prosperous and secure village was supposed to set a good example for other villages. The "splash of oil" system, with some modifications, has also been found useful by the United States in its efforts to pacify the same region in the middle of the twentieth century.

Indo-China produced rubber, opium, oil, zinc, and rice; and French colonists developed tea and coffee plantations in the highlands. But, like Africa, the economic benefits of the region could not be fully exploited until an effective transportation system was developed. The economic advantages of the Indo-Chinese empire must be weighed against the cost of pacification. The emergence of Japan as a modern, dynamic power in Asia impressed the Annamites and the Tonkinese. A spirit of Tonkinese nationalism flourished to such an extent that a number of insurrections took place in Tonkin in 1909. They were instantly suppressed, but the idea of a national liberation continued among the people.

French imperial expansion after 1870 was brought on by a number of factors, chief among which were commitments that had been made by earlier regimes in North Africa, Central Africa, and Southeast Asia. While Frenchmen worried about constitutional problems and German power, French expeditions were exploring the banks of the Congo and the Red River, and French businessmen were prospering in Tunisia and Cochin-China. Private enterprises and Church missions were often unsafe in regions where native political authority was crumbling. It was thus inevitable that the French government was called in to protect them. When the Third Republic was firmly established, public opinion became aware of French involvement in remote parts of the world, and imperialism became a political issue. On July 28, 1885, shortly after his ministry was overthrown because of its commitments in Indo-China, Jules Ferry gave a speech in the Chamber of Deputies in which he justified his policy on the grounds that colonies benefited France economically, that Europeans had a duty to civilize the inferior peoples of the world, and that such a policy was strategically sound in terms of French interests in the Mediterranean and in the Pacific. Actually, these arguments were offered to make it seem that what had taken place in Asia and in Africa was the result of conscious policy. But French imperialist expansion was the result of haphazard commitments and of the political instability in Africa and Asia that had prompted the government to act on behalf of private interests in these areas. In short, France built an empire before she developed an imperialist policy.

Ferry's argument that colonies were necessary for France's economic development had no foundation. In the 1880s, the economy was stagnant; French industry was barely able to meet the demands of the home market, and thus France was hardly in a position to look for foreign outlets. The tariffs that were erected to protect agriculture and industry were partially designed to protect them from competition from the colonies. French wine producers were much annoyed by the cheaper Algerian wines that were flooding the domestic market. French capital, a major export, was invested in government bonds or in Russian industry; relatively little went into the economic development of the colonies. Private enterprise, to be sure, flourished in Saigon, Tunis, and Algiers, but the economic advantages of the empire to the country as a whole were more than offset by the cost of administration and the maintenance of an effective military establishment for police purposes.

French imperialism, however, did serve a purpose in that it helped to revive French prestige. Though public opinion was

outraged by Ferry's war in Tonkin because it seemed so irrele-
vant, the French Empire remained, and Frenchmen learned to
be proud of their far-flung colonies. When the Fashoda Incident
occurred, many clamored for war with England, France's major
rival in Africa and Asia. The French territories in North Africa
had a strategic value as well, because they enabled France to
remain a major power in the Mediterranean. And it was because
of her Indo-Chinese empire that she became a major power in
Asia. The empire provided a training ground for the French
army, giving it valuable experience. Officers, such as Louis
Hubert Lyautey who was stationed in Indo-China and who was
chiefly responsible for the conquest of Morocco, were able to
serve their country in far-off places where they could forget
about Republican politics and the iniquities of the Dreyfus affair
and where their aristocratic paternalism could be exercised in
favor of "inferior" peoples. The empire also provided native
troops that were used to some advantage during World War I.
The importance of the empire to the French military establishment was made apparent after World War II, when it tried
desperately to hold on to the empire even to the point of re-
sisting the authority of Paris. But if the Second French Empire
helped to restore French prestige and honor, it also created
diplomatic problems that affected "European alliances and alignments."

FRENCH DIPLOMACY

German Chancellor Otto von Bismarck towered above
the European scene from 1870 until he was forced out of office
in 1890. As the most powerful nation on the continent, Germany
was able to take the diplomatic initiative, and the other powers
were forced to act accordingly. France was isolated in 1870, and
the Iron Chancellor saw to it that she remained so. In 1873,
the German government signed accords with Russia and Austria-
Hungary, making it difficult for France to find allies on the
continent; and in 1879, a defensive alliance was drawn up between Vienna and Berlin, becoming the first link of the Triple

Alliance. In 1881, Bismarck, unwilling to allow a discontented Russia to look for friends elsewhere, set up the League of the Three Emperors, which assured Germany of Russian neutrality in case of war between France and the Reich. At the Congress of Berlin in 1878, the German Chancellor encouraged France to occupy Tunisia, and his subsequent encouragement of French imperialism was intended not only to divert French attention from the continent, but also to generate antagonism between the Republic and Italy and Great Britain, all of whom had imperialist ambitions. In 1882, Italy became the third party in the Triple Alliance, driven there by the French occupation of Tunisia. And Anglo-French relations became strained at that time because of the establishment of British dominion over Egypt.

As a result of Bismarck's diplomacy, France was forced to confront Germany alone. Relations between the two countries were particularly tense because of the harsh provisions of the Treaty of Frankfurt. Thiers had been able to pay off the indemnity eighteen months ahead of time, and the French government began to reorganize the army after the defeat. A law passed in 1872 provided for universal military service with a term of service of five years; and in 1875, a law was enacted calling for the reorganization of the structure of the army by increasing the number of battalions.

The German government became alarmed because it believed that the law of 1875 facilitated mobilization. Rumors that the French were purchasing horses in Germany reached the High Command, and an embargo was placed on the export of horses. The "war scare" of 1875 was caused by German reaction to the rapid French recovery after the defeat and by Bismarck's fear that France might become a monarchy, thereby making it easier for her to find allies among the European powers. In fact, the Chancellor always supported the Republicans during the constitutional quarrels of the 1870s. Bismarck was also displeased at the attitude of some French bishops toward his *Kulturkampf*. The German press began to agitate, an editorial in the Berlin *Post* inquired whether war was imminent, and the French ambassador to Berlin heard talk in high places about a preventive war against France.

The French government considered setting aside the law of 1875, but the Minister of Foreign Affairs obtained assurances from England and Russia that they would not look kindly on a preventive war waged by Germany. The French government had at least received assurances that the European balance of power would prevent France from being entirely at the mercy of the empire across the Rhine, and it went ahead with reorganizing the army while Bismarck was forced to reconsider his whole policy toward his neighbor to the west.

In 1877, after the crisis of *seize mai,* relations between France and Germany improved. The Iron Chancellor was afraid that President MacMahon might establish a dictatorship with the support of political elements extremely hostile to the Reich; and he was pleased by the triumph of the Republicans, whom he regarded as having peaceful intentions. While Bismarck insisted upon keeping France isolated, he began to encourage colonial expansion by supporting French efforts in Tunisia in 1881 and in Indo-China in 1884, and by encouraging the Republic to take a firm line against England in Egypt. He even talked in terms of an alliance with France in 1884. In 1885, he invited French Premier Jules Ferry to confer with him either in Switzerland or in Luxemburg. Ferry appreciated German support of French imperialism, but he realized that public opinion would never permit a rapprochement with Germany without regaining Alsace-Lorraine, and he did not want to break with Great Britain despite the Egyptian situation. All of these considerations led him to decline Bismarck's invitation.

The fall of the Ferry ministry in 1885 revealed the extent of anti-imperialist sentiment in France, much of which was based on the belief that Ferry was playing Germany's game. Hostility toward the Reich was reflected in the activities of Déroulède's *Ligue des Patriotes* and in Boulanger's rise to power. The Schnaebelé incident indicated that relations between the two countries had again deteriorated to such an extent that

President Grévy in 1887 had to assure the German ambassador that he had personally removed Boulanger from his ministerial position. The French government was again made aware of its isolation.

The fall of Bismarck in 1890 had a stupendous effect on European diplomacy, if only because it meant that Germany lost the diplomatic initiative. After 1890, relations between the European capitals were no longer controlled as extensively by Berlin as they had been under the Iron Chancellor. France's ability to emerge from isolation meant that, for the first time since 1870, she was acting on her own initiative. Bismarck, it is true, was having difficulty toward the end of his tenure of office maintaining the Triple Alliance and the Reinsurance Treaty with Russia because of disagreements with her and with Austria-Hungary. Fritz von Holstein, who played a decisive role in German foreign policy after Bismarck's dismissal, decided that the Reinsurance Treaty was not in the interests of the Austro-Hungarian alliance and ought not to be renewed in 1890, a decision which forced a change in Russian foreign policy.

In order to prepare the way for an alliance between the two powers, the French government had been encouraging private investment in the Russian economy as well as private loans to the Czar's government, which was chronically in debt. Bismarck's efforts and Alexander III's aversion to the French Republic had prevented an alliance until 1890, when both Russia and France were faced with the possibility of isolation. The French Deputy Chief of Staff, who had been invited to observe the Russian military maneuvers in August 1891, was assured by Russian generals that in case of a German attack on France, the latter power could count on Russian support, and he heard vague references to the possibility of an alliance. The Russian government, however, did not seem to be in any hurry, much to the annoyance of the French government, which put pressure on the Rothschild Bank to refuse a Russian application for a loan. The Triple Alliance was renewed in 1891, and Russia became alarmed at the possibility that Great Britain had reached some sort of agreement with the Alliance powers about the Mediterranean. On August 5, a French naval squadron was fêted at Kronstadt, the Czar stood bare-headed while a band played the revolutionary *Marseillaise,* and the Russian foreign minister agreed to negotiate an alliance with the Third Republic.

France was primarily interested in military agreements, but the Russians refused to be too precise in discussing strategy. The two governments exchanged letters on August 27, 1891, agreeing to confer on all matters affecting world peace; if one of the countries was menaced by aggression, both would take steps to see what could be done to prevent it. France continued to press for a military pact until Alexander III finally agreed in July 1892 to allow French Chief of Staff Boisdeffre to come to Russia to negotiate with the Russian staff. The generals reached an agreement in August 1892 in which Russia promised to go to war against Germany or Italy supported by Germany if either or both attacked France, and France promised to declare war if Russia was attacked by Germany or by Austria-Hungary supported by Germany. Russia agreed to mobilize automatically if Germany mobilized against France, and France agreed to mobilize if Austria-Hungary *without* German support mobilized against Russia, thereby involving France in the tangled and dangerous Balkan situation.

The French government hesitated because it did not like the secret nature of the accords or the provision calling for mobilization against Austria. The Czar hesitated because the Panama Canal scandal, which was then reaching a crescendo, seemed to bear out the contention that the Republic was indeed decadent and not worth befriending. The Russian government even made overtures to Germany; but, receiving no encouragement from Berlin and annoyed by German tariffs on Russian imports, the Czar agreed to the military pact in December 1893. The French government, despite its reservations about the pact, followed suit in January 1894.

The Republic had finally emerged from the isolation imposed upon her by Bismarck, but the alliance with Russia was in no way regarded by the government or by responsible

public opinion as a means for France to adopt a more ag-
gressive foreign policy toward Germany. The idea of revenge for
the "rape" of Alsace-Lorraine was entertained by only a few
zealots such as Déroulède; but for most Frenchmen, the hope
of recovering the lost provinces (whose statues in the Place de
la Concorde remained draped in black), while not abandoned,
remained outside the realm of practical politics. The decade of
the 1890s, when the military pact with the Czar's government
was concluded, was also the decade in which the French
government with a good deal of popular support became increasingly committed to a policy of colonial imperialism. And,
as the French expanded in North Africa and in Indo-China, they
came into conflict with British interests. France had never for-
given her ancient enemy for gaining exclusive control over
Egypt in 1882, and she continued without success to press the
British government to pull out of that country. In Southeast
Asia, French and British interests came into conflict. As the
French pushed eastward from Annam into Cambodia and Laos,
they encountered opposition from Siam, a state which constituted a buffer zone between French Indo-China and British
Burma. The Siamese occupied Laos in 1885, but they were
gradually forced out by the French. The Siamese government
objected to the French occupation of Laos, and the British
government was uneasy about it as well. In July 1893, the
French sent gunboats up the Menam River to Bangkok to force
Siam to accept the *fait accompli*. The British government announced that it was gravely concerned; but it decided not to
intervene when it became clear that the independence of the
buffer kingdom was not in jeopardy, and the Siamese government backed down.

The major conflict between the two colonial powers occurred in 1898 on the Upper Nile. The French were interested
in expanding eastward with the intention of linking the West
African colonies to the French port of Djibouti on the Red Sea,
while the British were considering the possibility of linking
Cairo to Capetown by rail. A British military expedition under
General Kitchener moved south from Egypt to subdue a revolt in

the Sudan and to insure British control of the Upper Nile. In 1897, a small French military expedition led by Captain Marchand set out from Brazzaville in hopes of getting a foothold in the same region. If the French moved into the gap between British Uganda and the Sudan, not only would the possibilities of linking West and East African colonies be realized but the British would be thwarted in their efforts to link North and South Africa. Thus, a major reason for the British control of Egypt would be removed. In July 1898, the Marchand mission, after an extremely difficult march through the jungle, arrived at Fashoda on the Nile just below Khartoum. After capturing Khartoum from the rebellious Dervishes, General Kitchener moved south to Fashoda in September, forcing a showdown between the two powers. The British government, which had made its African intentions known as early as 1890 and had received the support of Germany, Italy, and Belgium in its efforts to build a railroad between Capetown and Cairo, had warned France in 1894 that it would regard a French mission to the Upper Nile as an unfriendly act. It now insisted that Marchand evacuate Fashoda. The French government, knowing that the expedition might cause a major international crisis, found its position to be untenable. It could not count on support from the other powers, the French navy was much inferior to that of Great Britain, and the Dreyfus affair was affecting its will to act. Therefore, Marchand was ordered to withdraw from Fashoda.

French foreign policy in the 1890s was forced to adjust to the problems raised by imperial expansion. French honor and prestige were more likely to be revived in Africa and in Asia than on the European continent, where German power provided an insurmountable obstacle, but an ambitious policy outside of Europe meant aggravating the historic rivalry with England. In the minds of some at the Foreign Ministry, increased rivalry with Great Britain meant reevaluating France's relations with Germany. Although Gabriel Hanotaux, the Minister of Foreign Affairs from 1894 to 1898, was unwilling to effect a permanent rapprochement with Berlin, he saw advantages to occasional cooperation with Germany, one of the advantages being to put pressure on Great Britain in Africa and Asia.

Théophile Delcassé, Minister of Foreign Affairs from 1898 until 1905, believed that France would never have a satisfactory relationship with the Reich until the lost provinces were returned. Delcassé had been the first Minister of Colonies in 1894, however, and he was closely associated with politicians who were constantly lobbying on behalf of colonial interests. When he moved to the Quai d'Orsay in 1898, Delcassé determined that the elimination of England from Egypt would be his main objective because her presence there was detrimental to French interests in the Mediterranean. However, after the Fashoda crisis, he concluded that this objective could not be fulfilled. At the same time, the French government began to consider the possibility of establishing dominion over Morocco, an undertaking which would require some sort of understanding with the British. Great Britain, involved in the unpopular Boer War, was becoming alarmed by Germany's hostile attitude and by her own isolation, and she was not unsympathetic to French overtures.

When President Loubet paid a state visit to London in July 1903, Delcassé proposed to Lord Landsdowne, the English Foreign Secretary, that the two countries should agree to an arrangement in North Africa. The result, the Entente Cordiale of 1904, was an agreement specifically relating to the imperial interest of the two countries involved. The French government recognized English control of Egypt while the British government gave France a free hand in Morocco. Ten years after the alliance with Russia, the French government had established a rapprochement with another major power that considerably enhanced her international status.

French diplomacy was successful not only in making the country more secure against the Triple Alliance, but it was also weakening that alliance by coming to terms with Italy. The secret agreement between Paris and Rome in July 1902 resembled the Anglo-French entente in that its main concern was North Africa. Rome agreed to accept France's right to "protect" Tunisia, while Paris agreed to permit a free hand for Italy in Lybia. At the same time, Italy agreed to remain neutral in the event of a war between France and Germany, even if France—because of serious provocation—declared war first.

In March 1905, Kaiser Wilhelm II stepped off his yacht in the Moroccan port of Tangiers and proclaimed himself Morocco's protector in her struggle to remain free of French control. This was not the rash act of an unstable and impetuous despot, but a carefully planned maneuver by the German government. The Entent Cordiale had excluded the Reich from the Moroccan arrangements on the grounds that Germany had no interest in the area. Wilhelm's speech at Tangiers was intended to assert a German interest in North Africa and to reiterate the Kaiser's desire for imperialist expansion in the underdeveloped areas of the world. The German government was also concerned about France's recent diplomatic successes and was anxious to regain the diplomatic initiative. By intervening in Morocco, Germany was testing the Entente Cordiale by challenging England to live up to her agreement to support France in Morocco. If British support was limited, then the two imperialist powers would again be at odds. Berlin also hoped to weaken the Franco-Russian Alliance. At the time, Russia was engaged in a war with Japan (Great Britain's ally), and St. Petersburg was not happy about France's understanding with London—Russia's rival in Asia and the Middle East. If England supported France in Morocco, Russia might consider abandoning her alliance with France, which would force Paris into a choice between London and St. Petersburg.

The *coup de Tanger* caused consternation in France. The government headed by Rouvier was anxious to avoid war because the country was deeply involved in domestic crises—the separation of church and state and the lingering problems of the Dreyfus affair. Rouvier agreed to accept an international conference on the Moroccan question, and Delcassé was forced to resign. The removal of Delcassé from the Quai d'Orsay represented a diplomatic triumph for Germany, because she regarded Delcassé as the man chiefly responsible for the Entente Cordiale and the weakening of the Triple Alliance. But the result of the first Moroccan crisis was very different from what was intended by the Kaiser's government. Great Britain supported the French position at the international conference that convened in Algeciras in Spain, and the British military staff was given permission to study the possibility of joint military action with France if the appropriate occasion arose. The Russian delegation also supported France at Algeciras. It proved to be Germany rather than France who was isolated by the crisis. France's position was immeasurably strengthened with the completion of the Triple Entente a year later when Great Britain and Russia agreed to settle their differences.

The first Moroccan crisis awakened most Frenchmen to the fact that Germany was a menace both on the European continent and in the race for colonies. Even those who before 1905 had considered the desirability of a limited rapprochement with Berlin reluctantly concluded that there might be another war with the German Empire. The policy of the French government after 1905 was to make the country as secure as possible by strengthening its system of alliances. France and Russia had a military agreement; but London, though willing to consider joint military and naval action with the French, would not state precisely in advance the conditions that would bring her into a war. With each crisis after 1905, the major powers sought to increase their security, dividing Europe gradually into two armed camps.

The German government, realizing that the Triple Entente was made up of three nations whose interests in Africa and Asia were often in conflict, continued its diplomatic offensive against it. During the summer of 1911, a French military expedition occupied the Moroccan city of Fez to quell disturbances. The Germans, considering such action a violation of the Algeciras accords, sent the gunboat *Panther* to the port of Agadir with the intention of frightening Paris into making concessions. Premier Joseph Caillaux, one of the diminishing number of Frenchmen who still believed that a conciliatory policy toward Germany was possible, sought to negotiate by offering concessions. In November 1911, the two powers reached an agreement whereby Germany finally recognized France's right to a free hand in Morocco, and the French agreed to cede some territory in the French Congo to Germany. French public opinion, proud of the empire and hostile toward Germany, was outraged, causing the downfall of the Caillaux ministry in January 1912, to be replaced by one headed by Raymond Poincaré, an advocate of a hard line toward the Reich.

The major trouble spot on the European continent was the Balkans, where the nationalist sentiments of the various ethnic groups and the competing interests of Austria-Hungary and Russia were creating an unstable situation. France's interest in the area was negligible, but her alliance with Russia forced her to become involved in the various crises that occurred after 1909. The first Balkan War, which began in October 1912, concluded with the Ottoman Empire being entirely forced out of southeastern Europe by Serbia, Rumania, Bulgaria, and Greece. However, quarreling among the victors brought on the second Balkan War in June 1913. The emergence of Serbia as a significant power in the region proved to be a source of contention between Russia and Austria. Russia regarded herself as the sponsor of Slavic movements and so supported Serbian ambitions; but the Dual Monarchy, which included Slavic minorities in the provinces of Bosnia and Herzogovina, regarded these ambitions as a threat to its integrity.

The allies of Russia and Austria—France and Germany, respectively—instead of seeking to reduce tensions in the Balkans by discouraging dangerous policies, strengthened their commitments to St. Petersburg and Vienna. Germany encouraged Austria to take a firm stand in southeastern Europe in order to sustain the Triple Alliance. France, by an agreement with Russia in July 1912, just before the first Balkan War, promised to support Russian interests in the troubled area—by military intervention if necessary—even though Poincaré disapproved of Czarist policy there. French investment capital was also used to promote Russian and Serbian interests. Because Austria felt threatened by the Balkan victory over Turkey, the German government decided to increase the size of its army in January 1913. This forced France to return to the Three-Year Law, which brought on domestic problems.

On June 28, 1914, Archduke Ferdinand, heir to the Hapsburg throne, was assassinated at Sarajevo; and the Austrian government, backed by Germany, undertook to punish Serbia, the sponsor of the plot. The Dual Monarchy declared war on Serbia on July 28, and Russia mobilized for war on July 30. On July 31, Germany issued ultimatums to Russia and France and at the same time issued its own mobilization decrees. The French government, headed by René Viviani, rejected the German ultimatum, which included the impossible demand that France surrender the fortresses of Toul and Verdun as proof of her desire to remain neutral; and, on the evening of August 1, the French army prepared for war. Germany declared war against Russia on August 1, and against France two days later. The invasion of Belgium on the same day brought England into the conflict on the side of France and Russia.

France did not want war in 1914. Despite the uneasiness about Germany and the revival of nationalist sentiments, the elections of April 1914 indicated a strong desire for peace on the part of the French people. The idea of a revanchist war with Germany over Alsace-Lorraine had little support in a country that had been soundly defeated in 1870. To what extent, then, is the Third Republic to be held responsible for the events that led to the holocaust in 1914? By becoming increasingly involved in colonial expansion, France contributed to the general atmosphere of international tension. Colonial expansion enlarged the area in which French interests would conflict with foreign interests; and, when Germany entered the competition for empire, the already poor relations between the two states deteriorated even further. The alliance with Russia was also partially responsible for the events of 1914. The French government, pleased by the security that the alliance provided, was encouraged to undertake an adventuresome foreign policy in Africa and Asia. More important, however, is the fact that French diplomacy between 1912 and 1914 put the interests of the alliance ahead of sound policy. Instead of attempting to reduce the tensions building up in the Balkans, Poincaré and others encouraged Russia to pursue a policy that would inevitably lead to conflict with Austria, even though Poincaré and others realized that the Czarist government's policy was not sound. They committed their country to military intervention, which only served to increase the tensions that led to war.

6 / The Revolt against Positivism

Napoleon III invited many of the world's dignitaries to the Exposition of 1867 to show off the progress made by France under the Second Empire. In 1878, shortly after the political crisis of *seize mai*, the French government sponsored an *Exposition Internationale*, but the list of distinguished guests included only the Shah of Iran and the Prince of Wales. The thousands of tourists who were attracted to Paris in that year were duly impressed by the recovery that France had made since the debacle of 1870–1871. But the Third Republic was still insecure, and so the "festival of the people" was held on June 30 instead of July 14 to prevent offending the sensibilities of the Right, and the band of the *Garde Républicaine* played the *Marseillaise* by special permission.

The Exposition of 1889 was intended not only to celebrate the centenary of the Great Revolution, but also the triumph of the Third Republic. It was held on the Champs de Mars and in the gardens of the Trocadero. The visiting dignitaries, including the accommodating Shah, the Prince of Wales, and King Leopold II of Belgium, were shown a statue on top of the Palace of Industry entitled "France Distributing Crowns to the Nations," and an illuminated fountain entitled "France Enlightening the World." They were given the opportunity to admire the colonial exposition at the Invalides where Senegalese, Algerian, and

Cochin-Chinese pavilions provided colorful testimony to the extent and diversity of the French Empire. The exposition paid tribute as well to French science and technology. Tourists were much impressed by the Gallery of the Machines, an enormous hall 420 yards long, 115 yards wide, and 45 yards high, constructed of steel and glass. The greatest monument to French technological ingenuity was the Eiffel Tower, which became a permanent landmark despite indignant protests from conservative Parisians. On top of the tower flew the tricolored flag, a symbol of progress under the Republic.

In 1900, the French government held another exposition to demonstrate to the world at large that France had successfully weathered the nineteenth century and was prepared to face the twentieth. It was held along the banks of the Seine, which had been "done over" to resemble the Grand Canal in Venice. In addition to the colonial pavilions, there was a "House of Mirth," a movie theater, and a "Theater of the Electric Dancer." The Boer Republics—Orange and the Transvaal—had pavilions to remind tourists of British brutality, and Germany was represented for the first time. The most popular tourist attraction was the Russian pavilion, the Czar's gift to the Republic. Visiting dignitaries to the Exposition included the King of Sweden and, once again, the Shah of Iran. Kaiser Wilhelm II, eager for a Franco-German rapprochement at the time, hoped to attend, but French sensibilities prevented it. The Exposition's permanent contributions to Paris, in addition to the first subway line, were the Gare d'Orsay, the Grand Palais, the Petit Palais, and the magnificent Alexander III bridge, symbol of the Franco-Russian Alliance.

France had placed a high value upon scientific accomplishments since the eighteenth century, and no regime was more conscious of the value of science than the Third Republic, whose expositions boasted the achievements of French scientists as well as those of the Republic. Between 1871 and 1914 France made significant contributions to science. One of the many outstanding scientists was Marcelin Berthelot, who made discoveries in the field of organic chemistry. His insistence that chemical phenomena are governed by universal laws did much to strengthen the mechanical view of the universe as well as of positivism generally. Berthelot was elected Senator for life in 1881; and between 1886 and 1887, he was Minister of Education. He was Minister of Foreign Affairs in 1898. Another noted Frenchman, Louis Pasteur, established the validity of the germ theory of disease; and in 1885, he successfully inoculated a child against hydrophobia. In 1874, the National Assembly voted Pasteur a life pension. In 1881, he was elected to the *Académie française*; and in 1887, he became permanent secretary to the *Académie des Sciences*. In 1888, the Institut Pasteur was founded with a private endowment and public funds to carry on the study of disease.

The mechanical conception of the universe as governed by universal laws with the atom as the smallest unit—a conception which had dominated scientific thought from Newton to Berthelot and was essential to positivism—was shattered by a number of discoveries at the turn of the century. These discoveries revolutionized physics and prepared the way for Einstein's theory of relativity, and France made substantial contributions to this new view of the universe. Henri Poincaré, cousin of Raymond, advanced the study of electromagnetic waves and undertook to conceptualize relativity in terms of mathematical formulae. Henri Becquerel discovered the radioactivity of uranium salts in 1896; and in 1898, Pierre and Marie Curie made their contributions to the Atomic Age by extracting two new elements, polonium and uranium, from pitchblende. In 1910, Jean Perrin, who began his career as a teacher at the prestigious *École Normale Supérieure,* was able to determine the size and number of atoms and molecules and to confirm the molecular nature of fluids.

French technology at the turn of the century was also impressive. It began with the bicycle, which played an important role in French life in the 1890s. The velocipede had been transformed in 1885 as a result of the discovery of the chain and adaption of two wheels. In 1891, Edouard Michelin invented the inner tube, making it easier to change flat tires;

and, by the turn of the century, the two-wheeled vehicle was available at popular prices. And in 1883, a Frenchman constructed the first automobile to be fueled by gasoline. In the following year a compatriot invented the six-cylinder motor. By 1889, a small automobile industry existed in France. An automobile reached the incredible speed of twenty-one kilometers an hour on the road between Paris and Rouen in 1894; and, in the same year, there were two hundred cars in the country.

In 1870, when Gambetta left Paris by balloon to organize an army to lift the siege, France entered the Air Age. Jules Verne's novels, enormously popular at the turn of the century, inspired countless budding French engineers and inventors to succeed where Daedalus had failed. On a plateau at Savory on October 14, 1897, Clément Ader flew a batlike machine, which he called an *avion*, two hundred yards. Wilbur Wright experimented with airplanes in France in 1908; and in 1909, the first *Salon de l'Aeronautique* was held at the Grand Palais. In the spring of that year a Frenchman flew from Douai to Arras, a feat followed on July 25 by Louis Blériot's flight from Calais to Dover, amazing and delighting the entire world.

The brothers Louis and August Lumière showed the first movie, entitled *Workers Leaving the Lumière Factory,* in 1895, and Georges Meliès made still greater contributions to cinematography. He built a studio at Montreuil-sous-Bois where everything was done to make the movie a form of art. In 1897, he produced *Joan of Arc,* a film 2727 meters long. Unfortunately, Meliès had no sense of business and was unable to capitalize on his invention; and by 1918 he was selling candy at the Montparnasse railway station in Paris.

Although France admired her scientists and technologists, she was not inclined to support them to the extent of providing them with proper facilities. The Curies worked in poorly equipped laboratories with no funds for research; and, when Pierre Curie became Professor of Physics at the Sorbonne in 1909, he was not provided with a laboratory. The Third Republic was more generous than the Second Empire, which had provided millions of francs for the construction of the Opera House in Paris but almost nothing to support Pasteur's endeavors. The Chamber of Deputies allotted 100,000 francs to the Institut Pasteur, thereby helping it to become self-supporting, but research facilities were meager in Paris and almost nonexistent in the provinces before 1914. Even the French educational system, so much under the influence of positivism, emphasized the humanities at the expense of the natural sciences. Serious efforts by the government to bring French science to a level with England, Germany, and the United States began after World War I.

Though the French government was reluctant to support scientific research and though the schools devoted too much time to the classics, French faith that the scientific method was the only means of acquiring knowledge remained strong between 1870 and 1914. Positivism, whose high priest was Auguste Comte, affected the politics as well as the art and literature of the period. Politicians, such as Jules Ferry, were eager, in the name of science, to purge the schools and universities of theological and metaphysical errors.

Two of the most influential intellectuals in France during the last quarter of the century were Hippolyte Taine and Ernest Renan, both of them thoroughly imbued with positivism and scientism. Taine, who began his literary career with a study of English literature, concluded that spiritual manifestations were as much products of soil and environment as "vitriol and sugar." His belief was that the literary historian must examine the same phenomena as the geographer. Profoundly disillusioned by France's defeat at the hands of Prussia, Taine undertook a study of modern French history, which resulted in the *Origins of Contemporary France* (1875–1885). He decided that the French people had been misled by the metaphysical and unrealistic principles of the Enlightenment, which had resulted in revolution and chaos. Borrowing from Burke, Taine argued that what the nation needed in 1789 was not revolution but reform of traditional institutions. The institutions of the Old Regime were products of soil and environment, whereas those after 1789 were based on abstractions.

Renan, who studied for the priesthood at the Seminary of Saint-Sulpice, was forced to renounce Christianity because it was unscientific: the existence of God was not demonstrable. His notorious *Life of Jesus,* published the year before the *Syllabus of Errors* of 1863, was an analysis of the life of a human being in terms of his environment. One of Renan's most influential works, written in 1849 but not published until 1890, was *The Future of Science,* in which he praised science for destroying myths and falsehood and expressed belief that science alone would one day resolve all the urgent problems confronting mankind. In this work, the former seminarian insisted on the importance of a scientific education and of state support in advancing research.

Between 1789 and 1870, Frenchmen wrote history to support their political convictions. After 1870, the influence of science on historiography was very strong. The Germans, primarily Leopold von Ranke, stressed the importance of a critical use of sources; and French historians, many of whom had studied in Germany, concluded that they could show a period of history "as it really was" by being thoroughly objective. Gabriel Monod, who founded the *Revue Historique* in 1875, combed the archives for materials relating to early French history, and Ernest Lavisse edited and contributed to that monument of objective historiography the multivolumed *Histoire de France* (1900–1912). The geographer Vidal de la Blache made substantial contributions to the study of history by stressing the importance of the environment on the economic and social development of a region.

Try as they might to eliminate political and religious bias from their works in the name of objectivity, French historians were only partially successful. Studies of the French Revolution written in the period reveal a strong tendency to interject contemporary political ideals into a study of the past. Taine and Augustin Cochin found it impossible to conceal their dislike for the events that took place between 1789 and 1799. Alphonse Aulard, the first to hold a chair at the Sorbonne endowed for the purpose of studying the Revolution, ransacked the archives to bring as much evidence as possible to bear on his studies, but his work reflects the prejudices and ideals of a Radical of the Third Republic. Jean Jaurès and Albert Mathiez laid emphasis on economic and social problems related to the revolutionary era, at the same time reminding their readers of the ideals of social democracy.

In May 1885, Victor Hugo, poet and Republican, died at eighty-three years of age. He was given a state funeral by the government, which honored him as the nation's greatest poet, but the Romantic Era of which he was so much a part was long past. Since 1848, French literature had stressed realism and naturalism. According to Edmond de Goncourt, one of the leading literary critics at the beginning of the Republic, the novel should be as objective as the history book. Gustave Flaubert, the greatest exponent of naturalism, died in 1880, but his work was carried on by Émile Zola, who attempted to bring the techniques of the laboratory to literature. In 1871, he began a series of novels under the general title of the *Rougon-Macquert, Histoire naturelle et sociale d'une famille sous le Second Empire,* the best known volume of which was *Nana,* published in 1879. Zola portrayed the terrible condition of the working class in industrial areas; and, like Flaubert, he depicted the shallowness and narrow-mindedness of the bourgeois mentality. Another writer of the period whose novels and short stories reflect the importance of objective evaluation was Guy de Maupassant. The influence of science is also to be found in the poetry of the 1870s. The Parnassian school, whose leader was Leconte de Lisle, strove to present an impersonal, detached view of things.

French painting in 1870 was also naturalistic. Gustave Courbet, Socialist and friend of Proudhon, tried to show the world as it was and not as it ought to be. The paintings of Harpignies, Bastien-Lepage, and Daubigny, much in demand after the Franco-Prussian War, attempted to copy nature down to the last detail in the tradition of Millet and the Barbizon school. The classical tradition, always strong in French art and literature, lingered on in the banal paintings of Bougereau and Meissonier. But in April 1874, a group of artists who were unable to show their paintings at the official salons held an exhibition in a private studio in Paris. The painters included Claude Monet, Paul Cézanne, Alfred Sisley, Edgar Degas, Berthe Morisot, and Camille Pissarro. Their canvases represented a revolution in modern painting. The critics and public were disgusted, declaring the exhibition to be a declaration of war on taste and beauty. One critic called the entire collection "impressionist," taking the name from a painting by Monet entitled *Impression du soleil levant.* One of the leaders of the new school was Édouard Manet, who had been shocking the art world for a number of years with his "realistic" versions of classical masterpieces. Two of his best-known works, *Le Déjeuner sur l'herbe* inspired by Giorgione and *Olympia* inspired by Titian, were exhibited in 1863 to the dismay of the public. Manet came to "impressionism" in the late 1860s as a result of his efforts to be as realistic as possible. But generally, the impressionists, although they adopted entirely new techniques, were very much influenced by science. Monet, Sisley, and Pissarro were offering an analysis of color in their canvases, while Degas was primarily interested in analyzing form and movement. To the impressionists, the artist must represent the external world at the moment he becomes aware of it through his senses and before he can distort it with subjective or metaphysical considerations. Hence, a painting of an outdoor scene should be completed on the spot. In 1876 and 1877, other impressionist exhibitions were offered to a slightly more enthusiastic public; and in 1879, Renoir was able to show his *Portrait de Madame Charpentier et ses enfants* at the official salon. By 1890, impressionism was a generally accepted art form. One might say that the acceptance of impressionism occurred at the same time as the acceptance of the Republic, the intimate relationship between them being expressed in Monet's colorful *Rue de Montorgueil,* painted to celebrate the first Bastille Day holiday in 1879.

The influence of positivism in all phases of French life was particularly strong between 1870 and 1890, but one should not underestimate its influence after 1890. Émile Durkheim, who became Professor of Social Sciences at the Sorbonne in 1902 and was one of the pioneers of sociology in the twentieth century, always acknowledged his debt to Comte. A scientific study of society was perfectly possible, according to Durkheim; and a statistical analysis of birth, marriage, and suicide rates would provide much insight into the nature of a given society as well as into the relationship between the individual and society. In short, there is much about social development that is capable of measurement. Charles Maurras, borrowing from Taine, thought that a scientific analysis of French history revealed the necessity of a return to monarchy. Even the avant-garde playwright Alfred Jarry, involved as he was in the revolt against positivism, in 1898 invented "Pataphysics," the scientific study of the absurd.

ARTISTS AND INTELLECTUALS IN REVOLT

The revolt against positivism and naturalism began in art and literature as early as the 1870s, but its effect on French culture became strong in the 1890s. There are a number of reasons for the revolt. Artists came to feel that objectivism tended to restrict their ability to express themselves and that what was important in art was not the external world, but the world within the self. The artistic revolt at the end of the nineteenth century was somewhat similar to the Romantic revolt against the strictures of neo-classicism. The materialistic values of the bourgeoisie were identified with positivism in the minds of many intellectuals who emphasized the need for spiritual values. The economic recession of the 1880s and the poor living conditions of the working class seemed to belie the positivist-inspired belief in progress that was dear to hearts of Gambetta's followers. German culture, with its emphasis on idealism, was very influential in France after 1870, which explains the impact of Nietzsche on the French mind in the 1890s. That apocalyptic philosopher called for values created by the individual in his efforts to fulfill his highest potential. He rejected values imposed on the individual by the external world, either in the form of natural law or social convention. Nietzsche's appeal for self-expression was heard not only by the French intellectual community but also apparently by the anarchists, whose devastating bombs defied all authority. Finally, the dramatic discoveries of the mathematicians and physicists, which destroyed the cherished conception of a mechanical universe, weakened the influence of scientism.

The philosophical assault on positivism was undertaken by Henri Bergson, born of a prosperous Jewish family. He was a classmate of Jean Jaurès at the *École Normale Supérieure*. After a few years of teaching in provincial *lycées* and at the *École Normale*, Bergson was awarded the chair of philosophy at the *College de France*, where his exciting lectures attracted scholars, tourists, and the fashionable set. Shortly thereafter, he was elected to the *Académie française* and won the Nobel Prize for literature. Bergson contended that science provided an artificial view of nature and that reason distorted reality. In the tradition of Pascal, he emphasized the spiritual and the sentimental at the expense of the intellect. In a major work, *Creative Evolution,* published in 1907, he argued that it was intuition and not reason that came to grips with reality and perceived the vital impulse, the *élan vital,* which pervaded all of life. Thus, at a time when Freud was discovering the power of the subconscious and the irrational as motivating factors from the point of view of the clinician, Bergson, quite independently, was discovering it from the point of view of the philosopher.

Bergson's influence, on the eve of the war, was considerable. His emphasis on action and spontaneity caused military strategists, such as Colonel Foch at the *École Militaire,* to revise their approach to war by stressing offensive rather than defensive tactics. Bergson, though not a Catholic, contributed to the religious revival that took place at the turn of the century as part of the revolt against positivism and anticlericalism. In the 1880s, it was difficult for an intellectual to call himself a Catholic; but by 1914, religion was recognized as a vital spiritual force. Musicians like Vincent D'Indy revived interest in sacred music. In 1912, the young playwright and diplomat Paul Claudel published his *L'Annonce faite à Marie,* a medieval mystery play;

Georges Rouault applied modern painting techniques to religious themes, while the philosopher Jacques Maritain turned to St. Thomas Aquinas for spiritual guidance.

Bergson's philosophy was part of a general intellectual and artistic movement that stressed the subconscious, the mystical, and the primitive in opposition to the rationalism that was equated with the smug complacency of bourgeois civilization at the end of the nineteenth century. The symbolist school—including Stephane Mallarmé, Paul Verlaine, Jules Laforgue, and, all too briefly, the *enfant terrible* Arthur Rimbaud before he departed for the jungles of Africa—emerged in the 1870s and 1880s to carry on the poetic tradition of Charles Baudelaire. The symbolists believed that words should reflect the depths of the poet's soul rather than express clear and distinct ideas. Mallarmé felt that poetry should permit the reader to guess, to intuit, the poet's meaning and not provide him with a precise definition of external objects. Guillaume Apollinaire emerged as a leading poet between 1909 and 1918. His verse is impregnated with ambiguities and subtle meanings, and the distinctions between the personal and the universal, the external world and the artist's personality, break down completely.

The French novel also reflects the growing aversion to positivism. Anatole France carried on the skeptical tradition of Bayle and Voltaire by rejecting absolutes, while Pierre Loti sought to remove the reader from the humdrum world of the Republic to the exotic Orient. Paul Bourget, one of the leaders of the anti-Dreyfusard intellectuals, published a novel called *Le Disciple* in 1889, which stressed the moral irresponsibility of science, a theme very different from the one projected a year later by Renan in his *L'Avenir de la Science*. Maurice Barrès' *Les Désracinés*, published in 1897, portrayed young students becoming demoralized because of the positivist teaching in the French schools. André Gide, whose literary career began in the decade before the war, stressed the importance of intuition and psychology in understanding man's nature. Like Freud, Gide objected to the deleterious effect of social convention on the human being; but, being deeply imbued with the French classical heritage, he also emphasized the importance of form in art. In 1913, Marcel Proust retired to a cork-lined room to begin his monumental *A la Recherche du temps perdu,* in which the sub-conscious rather than the intellect proves to be the surest guide to understanding the past.

French painters abandoned the objective approach to nature in the 1880s. Vincent van Gogh's canvases, though influenced by the impressionists, reflected his own impressions and per-sonality in the exaggerated use of color rather than in an analysis of the external world. The primitivism of Henri Rousseau and Paul Gauguin seem to mock the achievements of nineteenth-century French civilization in much the way that Jean-Jacques Rousseau had mocked the accomplishments of his own time in his *Discourse on the Arts and Sciences.* Oriental art contributed much to the posters of Toulouse-Lautrec. The impact of primi-tivism and foreign cultures on French art and literature was partly the result of French colonialism, just as the earlier age of exploration affected the art and literature of the seventeenth and eighteenth centuries. The weird paintings of Puvis de Chavannes, Gustave Moreau, and Odilon Redon explored the world of dreams at a time when Freud and Bergson were just beginning their careers. A second revolution in French painting took place during the first decade of the present century. The public became aware of it at an exhibition at the Salon d'Automne that included works by Henri Matisse, Georges Rouault, Raoul Dufy, and Maurice Vlaminck. Furious critics used the epithet *fauves* (wild beasts) to refer to these painters, whose violent use of color and distorted forms represented the complete subordina-tion of the external world to the creative genius of the artist. The cubist school, which included Pablo Picasso, who came to Paris from Spain, Georges Braque, Juan Gris, and Fernand Léger, and whose sponsor was the poet Apollinaire, made itself known to Paris and the world in 1910. This school focused on the shifting appearances of geometric form and was clearly influ-enced by the theory of relativity, which had done so much to shatter the Newtonian conception of the universe.

The twentieth century owes much to French political

thought as well as to the art and literature of the period. The problems arising from industrialization and urbanization, the Dreyfus affair, and the regime itself were all subjected to the same penetrating analysis that light and form received from French painters. But the Third Republic had few supporters among the political theorists who made reputations for themselves. Among the best known was Émile-Auguste Chartier, a professor of philosophy at a Parisian *lycée* who wrote a number of pamphlets and newspaper articles in defense of radicalism under the pseudonym of "Alain." He believed the tyranny of government was always to be feared, and therefore the voters must keep a watchful eye on the deputies who might become so tempted by political power that they would forget their obligations to those who elected them to office. According to Alain, citizens should use the ballot as their ancestors had used the barricades—to protect themselves against abuses of authority. The political institutions of the Republic—with executive power weak and local interests strong—were in keeping with Alain's principles and those of thousands of small shopkeepers, lawyers, and doctors throughout rural France who wanted to remain free from governmental interference.

Charles Péguy was one who believed that what France needed was a Republic that would unite all the best traditions from Christianity to socialism. Born into a poor family in Orléans and a scholarship student at the *École Normale,* Péguy found himself passionately involved on the side of Dreyfus along with other *normaliens.* The Dreyfusard campaign had the same effect on young intellectuals that the barricades had for revolutionaries. The campaign seemed to have a cathartic effect, bringing the Republic alive by reminding it of its great heritage. From Péguy's point of view, if that sense of exhilaration could be sustained, the Republic would succeed, where other regimes had failed, to draw together all that was beautiful and noble in French civilization. What Péguy felt in the struggle to vindicate the unfortunate captain was a *mystique* that bound him and others together in a common cause.

But the Republic failed to keep that *mystique* alive. It became corrupt, and its politicians appeared interested only in "political games" and not in the spiritual welfare of the country. Péguy became a Socialist because he believed that socialism would heal the wounds that had plagued France since 1789, but he soon rejected the party of Jaurès because he thought that the Socialist *mystique* was being ground down by the machinery of the Republic. The Socialists were wrong in becoming involved in the anticlerical campaign, because it was only dividing the country even more. Péguy ultimately turned to Catholicism, believing that the religion of Joan of Arc, which had done so much to revive the nation in the fifteenth century, was what was needed in the twentieth century. Péguy died rather appropriately in the Battle of the Marne in the full flush of *union sacrée;* and, although his writings were rather neglected in the interwar period, they have aroused interest recently because one of his admirers, Charles de Gaulle, is carrying on his quest for a unifying *mystique.*

Among others who experienced disillusionment after the Dreyfus affair was Georges Sorel. Trained at the *École Polytechnique,* another prestigious school, Sorel was eminently successful as an engineer until he suddenly decided to resign his job in order to begin another career as a writer. Like Péguy, he was constantly in search of a just cause, which led him to adopt Marxism briefly in the 1890s and which caused him to flirt with the *Action française* for a time. Sorel admired "the makers and doers" of the world and not the talkers. He believed what the world needed was action and not theory. He hated the Republic because it was incapable of acting, incapable of inspired leadership. As a Socialist, he deplored the endless debates over principles, preferring instead the tactics of the trade unions that called for action in the form of strikes. In his best-known work, *Reflections on Violence,* published in 1908, he developed the concept that the myth is not so much a description of things as it is the expression of the will to act. In all ages, men had been inspired to act by myths—such as the coming of the Kingdom of God, the Holy Grail, and Liberty, Equality, Fraternity. What was needed in the contemporary age was another myth to inspire the new elite—the proletariat—to act in its own interest and in the interest of all mankind. The myth of the General Strike, which would bring the industrial world to a grinding halt, was what the workers needed instead of the interminable debates in the Chamber of Deputies. Violence was advocated by Sorel because it was a purifying force, a moralizing influence. This was especially true in an age of political decadence. It is little wonder that the practitioners of violence in our century, the Fascists and Communists, claim inspiration from Georges Sorel.

Maurice Barrès also believed that what his country needed was purification. Born in Lorraine, he left for Paris at the age of twenty; and, although he rarely left the capital, his heart remained in the provinces. Barrès is best known for his numerous novels, which, in addition to *Les Désracinés,* include *L'Appel au Soldat* and *Le Jardin de Bérénice;* but he was also a politician of sorts, having been elected to the Chamber in 1889 as a Boulangist from Nancy and again in 1906 as a representative of Paris. Like Péguy and Sorel, Barrès shifted across the political spectrum. In 1889, he regarded himself as a "nationalist socialist," a man of the Left; but in 1906, he saw himself as a Conservative because the Right had assumed the nationalist stance. According to Barrès, during the Napoleonic era, when French armies, inspired by patriotism, dominated Europe, France had been a dynamic nation. Under the Third Republic, the nation had become content with mediocrity. How could the Republic, governed as it was by Jews, Protestants, and Freemasons, restore France to its preeminent position in the world? What the country needed was a Man on Horseback—if not Boulanger, then someone else who would provide the necessary leadership and rekindle the flame of nationalism. Nationalism provided strength and energy because it evoked a common culture, a common tradition. Nationalism was also a purifying force because it rid the body politic of foreign elements—such as the Jews, whose traditions were different and whose blood was poison. Barrès passionately defended the army's right to sustain Dreyfus' conviction. No member of an alien race could be trusted; and, therefore, Dreyfus must be guilty. These views, eloquently expressed in novels and essays, unquestionably contributed to the Fascist cult of racial superiority.

Charles Maurras also believed in racial and national integrity. Where Barrès sought another Bonaparte to rise and lead the people, Maurras called for a return to the monarchy. He was certain that only the House of France was capable of understanding the national interest, because it had been identified with it since the days of Hugh Capet in the tenth century. Only the king was capable of rising above the din of parliamentary squabbles to unify the country by reviving the institutions of the Old Regime and by purging it of foreign elements. But the events of the 1870s had made it clear to the meanest intelligence that the monarchy could not be restored by legal procedure. And so, like Sorel and Barrès, the founder of the *Action française* advocated violence and revolutionary action.

French political thought at the turn of the century was as much an expression of revolt against positivism as of disgust with the Republic. The ideas expressed by Péguy, Sorel, and Barrès had much in common with the art and literature of the period. Sorel and Maurras intended to shock the sensibilities of the bourgeoisie (*épater le bourgeoisie*) in the same way that Apollinaire, *les fauves,* and even the inventor of the can-can—which was outlawed by the government—hoped to shock. The gross figure of Alfred Jarry's King Ubu, who first strutted onto the stage in 1896 and whose first word was "merde," was just as outrageous as Sorel's *Reflections on Violence* to the mentality that believed in the sweet reasonableness of things and the law of progress. The *avant-garde* artists who wanted to break down the barriers that separated art and life placed the same emphasis on action that the political theorists did, and the cult of the absurd reinforced the contempt that many intellectuals held for the Republic. The abrupt sounds of Stravinsky's *Sacre du Printemps,* which infuriated Paris in 1913, and the use of color by Matisse and Léger reveal the same attraction to violence exemplified by Sorel, Maurras, and the bomb-throwing anarchists in the political realm. The artists and musicians who flourished in Paris at the turn of the century were anxious to destroy the consecutiveness, the natural and harmonic progression that was characteristic of traditional are forms, just as intellectuals wanted to destroy the cherished belief that progress was inevitable.

The period between 1885 and 1914 was a period of remarkable cultural vitality in France and more particularly in Paris. One important reason for this vitality was the increased opportunity available for writers, painters, and musicians in an age when democratic education was making intellectual and cultural awareness more widespread. An artist no longer had to worry about offending the tastes of a drawing-room elite. The salon, so essential to the development of French culture, continued to flourish until around 1900. The Princess Mathilde Bonaparte entertained Anatole France, Proust, and others in her house in the Rue de Berri and Mme. Aubernon entertained "the wits" in her salon in the Rue D'Astorg, where she alone determined the topic of conversation. But it was the bistro and café that were becoming the main rendezvous of intellectuals. The *Action française* movement began at the Café Flore, and the Lapin Agile in Montmartre was crucial to the success of the *avant-guarde* movement. The desire for free expression and the exhilaration that pervades the art and literature of the period is in part the result of the artists' sense of relief at being able to escape the salon to mingle with the crowd in the street cafés. This exhilaration is also explained partly by the intellectuals' recent awareness that they were among the leaders of a free society. The Dreyfus affair was a clear indication of the extent to which the intellectual had become involved in the life of the community as a whole. There was criticism of this involvement, some of it from Julien Benda, who—in his influential book *Le Trahison des clercs,* published shortly after the war—argued in favor of greater detachment on the part of the intellectual elite.

Yet there was a strong sense of dissatisfaction and frustration within the French intellectual and artistic community at the turn of the century. Political theorists disliked the smug complacency of bourgeois society and the mediocrity of the regime, and their writings reflect a feeling of alienation. Sorel's exaltation of the myth and Barrès exaltation of the nation were efforts on the part of both to bring about the kind of society in which they could live on a mutually constructive basis. At the same time, painters and poets were dissatisfied with established art forms and sought to express themselves in new ways. The tension that existed between the intellectuals and the regime, together with the tension that existed between artists and established art forms, contributed substantially to the cultural dynamism of France during *la belle époque*.

7 / "The Good Old Days"

Looking back at the era before World War I, Frenchmen like to refer to it as *"la belle époque,"* which roughly translated means "the good old days." The French were not the only people to look back on those years with nostalgia. Americans called it "the gilded age," and President Warren G. Harding promised in 1920 that his administration would, in effect, turn the clock back. Of course it was impossible for anyone to "return to normalcy," to re-create the conditions that existed at the turn of the century. The United States and the European countries, in addition to coping with the problems created by the war, also had to cope with the problems arising from the accelerated pace of industrialization and urbanization. Frenchmen, confused and angry because of the rapid transformations taking place around them, allowed their memories to take them back to a simpler era when there seemed to be greater social and political stability.

There was some justification for this romantic yearning for the good old days. After almost a century of political upheaval, France had finally established a regime that was admirably suited to its social structure. "The Republic," said Thiers in 1873, "would be conservative, or it would not be." By this he meant that the Third Republic would have to adopt institutions that would be acceptable to a significant element of the political Right. The Constitutional Laws of 1875, with their emphasis on a dominant bicameral legislature and a weak executive, reflected a compromise between Orléanists and conservative Republicans. But Thiers also meant that the Republic would have to abandon its revolutionary heritage. By 1905, most Republicans—including that old Radical, Clemenceau—believed that the revolutionary goals had been achieved. Universal manhood suffrage and free, compulsory primary education were secured; civil rights were strengthened; and the separation of church and state had been accomplished. These goals had been set forth in a pre-industrial age, and they were finally achieved more than a century later by small-town lawyers and doctors who did not entirely understand the problems of industrialization and urbanization or the effect these problems had upon the revolutionary principles of "Liberty, Equality, Fraternity." When the Socialists argued that the French Revolution was unfinished and when the syndicalists argued that they were the true heirs of the Jacobins, the Republicans became alarmed by the possibility that all they and their ancestors had worked for might become undone by continued agitation from the Left.

By the turn of the century, Opportunists and Radicals had become defenders of the status quo, which included not only political democracy but also property rights and the interests of rural France. Anticlericalism, which was a revolutionary issue at the end of the eighteenth century, was used at the end of the nineteenth century to obscure pressing economic and social problems and to mask the conservative evolution of yesterday's radicals. The alliance with Czarist Russia, which signaled the end of French isolation, also symbolized Republican repudiation of the revolutionary ideal. By 1914, there was a distinct possibility that a conservative party dedicated to the preservation of social and political order might come into being as more Conservatives reluctantly abandoned hope of changing the regime, as more Republicans became conservative, and as pressure from the Socialist and Syndicalist Left increased.

What is most striking about France at the turn of the century is the influence of tradition on French society and institutions despite the revolutionary upheavals that took place between 1789 and 1871. The bourgeoisie and the peasants, who had the most to gain from the Revolution of 1789, continued to have great influence on political life after 1871, but their values were largely shaped by the traditions of the Old Regime. The aristocracy, weakened but certainly not destroyed by the revolutions, continued to dominate the social life of Paris and the provinces just as they had in the seventeenth and eighteenth centuries. The Dreyfus affair was caused, in part, by conflicting values: those who defended the army against the Dreyfusards invoked the principles of "military honor" and "reason of state," indicating that such values closely associated with the Old Regime were very much alive. The French educational system, which owed much to the Revolution, still emphasized a traditional curriculum at the expense of science and technology. Relatively free from the pressures of a rapidly increasing population, protected by tariffs and by political institutions designed to resist change, French society might have stagnated had it not been for World War I and its aftermath.

The revolutionary tradition did not die out, however, after the defeat of the Commune. It was kept alive by various political and social groups that had little or nothing to gain from the status quo. Socialists and Syndicalists took pride in the fact that the Jacobin mantle had fallen on their shoulders, and they employed dogma, myths, oratory, and violence to keep the revolutionary flame alive. But the Left was not alone in keeping that tradition alive. Certain elements of the Right, frustrated by the failure of General Boulanger and by the success of the Dreyfusards, cherished the dream of overthrowing existing institutions. Bonapartism was a product of the French Revolution, but it had become a part of the French Right because of its authoritarian nature and because of the conservative views of many nineteenth-century Bonapartists. Bonapartism, however, thrived on popular support, which it obtained from plebiscites and the nationalist tradition. Although Napoleon III's supporters had suffered initial setbacks immediately after the fall of the Second Empire, they were able to acquire growing influence on the Right as a whole after 1875. Bonapartists stressed the importance of a strong leader, and they were highly critical of parliamentary institutions. Their appeal to national honor attracted Monarchists and popular elements alike as the economic depression of the

1880s set in, as the Republic seemed from their point of view to wallow in a mire of corruption, and as the German menace continued to assert itself. The Right almost succeeded in staging a revolution with popular support in 1888. Although it failed, the idea of a revolution from the Right was kept alive in the hearts of some Monarchists and Bonapartists who refused to rally to the Republic. Their anti-republicanism was sustained by the Dreyfus affair, by the *Action française*, and by the novels of Maurice Barrès. The radical Right drew popular support by appealing to nationalism at a time when the Left was abandoning it as a revolutionary principle; it fanned the flames of anti-Semitism and displayed a "social conscience" that it accused the Republicans of not having. The revolutionary tradition was not only kept alive by the syndicalist Left and the radical Right, but it was also very much in evidence in the revolt against positivism, in which artists and intellectuals appealed to action and violence in their efforts to undermine the values of the bourgeois Republic.

The continued existence of the revolutionary ideal indicated that there were pockets of discontent despite the stability of the regime. It also indicated that change, motivated by gradual industrialization and urbanization, was taking place despite precautions taken against it. The Third Republic was no more universally loved than were the other regimes that had come into existence since 1789. Syndicalist ardor, however, was frustrated by the resistance of employers and by the use of troops by the government. After 1910, there were signs that syndicalism was being abandoned by the trade union movement. At the same time, the nationalist revival after the first Moroccan crisis in 1905 stole some of the thunder from the radical Right, whose appeal remained limited between 1905 and 1914. French society was stable enough, and the Republic was secure enough to dampen revolutionary enthusiasm. This accounts for the fact that the regime by 1914 had lasted far longer than any other since the Revolution. But the frustrations continued, as did the revolutionary ideal, in muted form. As the Third Republic suffered the shocks of war and the upheavals of the inter-war period, the revolutionary ideal flared up again on the Left, encouraged by the Russian Revolution, and on the Right, encouraged by the emergence of fascism in Italy, Germany, and Spain—a movement which France had helped to generate in the pre-war era. There is more than a modicum of truth in the saying that the Fascist-oriented Vichy Regime established in 1940 represented the ultimate triumph of the anti-Dreyfusards.

Critics from the Left and Right accused the Republic of ineffectual leadership. The history of the twentieth century has shown that governments with strong executive power are necessary to deal with the complex foreign and domestic issues of our time. Reacting sharply against the personal rule of Napoleon III, the National Assembly in 1875 endowed France with a regime dominated by the legislature. The legislature in turn was dominated by local interests to such an extent that it was impossible to establish a homogeneous majority in the Chamber capable of sustaining a ministry. Ministerial instability was a chronic problem under both the Third and the Fourth Republics. Certainly, it reflected the nineteenth-century preference for limited government as well as the desire to protect vested interests, but it was particularly ill-suited to the problems of the twentieth century. Alexis de Tocqueville, one of the greatest French political thinkers, complained that French liberty was being destroyed by over-centralization, that local interests, since the Old Regime, had been sacrificed to the national interest. The French administration was remarkably centralized, reflecting the aims and aspirations of Colbert and Napoleon. Local government was dominated by the prefect, who was responsible to Paris. The institutions of the Third Republic, however, provided a check to bureaucratic centralization by enabling local interests to dominate. A political stalemate was thus achieved, discouraging effective government in the critical times after 1914.

Bibliography

The most comprehensive history of the Third Republic to date is Jacques Chastenet, *Histoire de la Troisième République* (Paris, 1952–62), 7 volumes. Others include Charles Seignobos, *L'Évolution de la Troisième République* (Paris, 1921); volume 8 of Ernest Lavisse, *Histoire de France Contemporaine,* dated but useful for factual detail; D. W. Brogan, *The Development of Modern France, 1870–1940* (New York, 1940), a lively account of the politics of the period, although weak on economic, social, and cultural aspects; Guy Chapman, *The Third Republic of France: The First Phase, 1871–1894* (London, 1962), a confused jumble of detail; David Thomson, *Democracy in France* (London, 1952), still the best synthesis of the political system and social structure of France under the Republic. Edward M. Earle, ed., *Modern France* (Princeton, 1951), and Stanley Hoffman *et al., In Search of France* (Cambridge, Mass., 1963), both contain valuable essays on political, social, and economic problems relating to the period. Two valuable works on the political evolution of the Republic are François Goguel, *La Politique des partis sous la Troisième République* (Paris, 1957), and A. Soulier, *L'Instabilité ministèrielle sous la Troisième République* (Paris, 1939). Adrien Dansette, *Histoire religieuse de la France contemporaine* (Paris, 1951), 2 volumes, is a useful survey of church-state problems since the Revolution of 1789. E. Beau de Loménie, *Les Résponsibilités des dynasties bourgeoises* (Paris, 1943–1960), 4 volumes, attempts to show that French politics were controlled by the major financial and industrial interests throughout the nineteenth and twentieth centuries. His thesis, although interest-

135

ing, is not entirely acceptable for the period under consideration in this book. Badly needed are regional studies of France during the past two centuries because local issues were of paramount importance in the political life of France. Pierre Barral, *Le Département de l'Isère sous la Troisième République* (Paris, 1962), represents a good beginning in this direction.

There are innumerable studies of specific political events, problems, and groups during the period between 1870 and 1914. Of the many works on the Paris Commune, Karl Marx, *The Civil War in France* (Moscow, 1948), one of the author's most important works, is a classic Marxian analysis of a revolutionary event; Edward S. Mason, *The Paris Commune* (New York, 1930), attempts to destroy the "Socialist mythology" in order to understand the forces at work in the Commune; Frank Jellinek, *The Paris Commune of 1871* (New York, 1965), presents a modified Marxist view of the Commune. Jean T. Joughin, *The Paris Commune in French Politics, 1871–1880* (Baltimore, 1955), is useful. Daniel Halévy, *La Fin des notables* (Paris, 1930), and *La République des ducs* (Paris, 1939), are studies of the political origins of the Republic by one who was very much involved in French political life before 1914. Other significant monographs on French politics of the period include Evelyn Acomb, *The French Laic Laws, 1879–1889* (New York, 1941); Adrien Dansette, *Le Boulangisme* (Paris, 1946) and *Les Affaires de Panama* (Paris, 1934); Alexander Sedgwick, *The Ralliement in French Politics, 1890–1898* (Cambridge, Mass., 1965); L. V. Méjan, *La Séparation des églises et de l'état* (Paris, 1959); Jacques Chastenet, *La France de M. Fallières* (Paris, 1946); and Eugen Weber, *The Nationalist Revival in France, 1905–1914* (Berkeley, 1959). Of the numerous works on the Dreyfus affair, of particular value are Guy Chapman, *The Dreyfus Case* (London, 1955); Douglas Johnson, *France and the Dreyfus Affair* (London, 1966); and Pierre Miquel, *L'Affaire Dreyfus* (Paris, 1959). Robert F. Byrnes, *Antisemitism in Modern France* (New Brunswick, N.J., 1950), examines the roots of French anti-Semitism, but unfortunately stops short of the Dreyfus affair. Hannah Arendt, *The Origins of Totalitarianism* (Cleveland, 1962), is essential to an understanding of anti-Semitism. Jacques Kayser, *Les Grandes batailles du radicalisme, 1820–1901* (Paris, 1962), is a study of the political origins of Radicalism. Aaron Noland, *The Founding of the French Socialist Party* (Cambridge, Mass., 1956), and Robert Wohl, *French Communism in the Making* (Stanford, 1966), are among the best surveys of the French Socialist movement before World War I, as is Leslie Derfler, "Le Cas Millerand: une nouvelle interpretation," *Revue d'Histoire Moderne et Contemporaine X* (April–June, 1963), pp. 81–104. Indispensable to an understanding of the French Right is René Rémond, *La Droite en France* (Paris, 1954), and Eugen Weber's essay on the French Right in E. Weber and H. Rogger, ed., *The European Right* (Berkeley and Los Angeles, 1965) provides new insight into the radical tendency. Eugen Weber, *Action française* (Stanford, 1962), and Ernste Nolte, *Three Faces of Fascism* (New York, 1966), are important contributions to the history of the revolutionary tendency within European conservatism in the present century. Another contribution to the growing body of literature on the French Right is Samuel Osgood, *French Royalism under the Third and Fourth Republics* (The Hague, 1960). Henri Rollet, *L'Action sociale des catholiques en France, 1870–1901* (Paris, 1947), and Maurice Vaussard, *Histoire de la démocratie chrétienne* (Paris, 1956), examine Catholic responses to "the social question."

There are a number of books and articles on the economic history of France between 1870 and 1914. J. H. Clapham, *The Economic Development of France and Germany, 1815–1914* (Cambridge, 1936), is dated but still useful both for factual information and as a comparative study. Charles P. Kindleberger, *Economic Growth in France and Britain, 1851–1950* (Cambridge, Mass., 1940), adopts the same comparative approach to economic development, and applies modern concepts of economic growth to economic history. Rondo Cameron, *France and the Economic Development of Europe, 1800–1914* (Chicago, 1955), stresses the importance of French finance capital to the economic development of Europe. Shepard B. Clough, *France: A History of National Economics* (New York, 1939), and Eugene Golob, *The Méline Tariff* (New York, 1941), are studies of the role of the

French government in the economic life of the country, as is Michel Augé-Laribé, *La Politique agricole de la France de 1880 à 1940* (Paris, 1950). Another contribution to modern French agricultural history is Charles K. Warner, *The Winegrowers in France and the Government since 1875* (New York, 1960). Significant articles on the French economic history of the period include Rondo Cameron, "Economic Growth and Stagnation in France, 1815–1914," *Journal of Modern History*, XXX (1958), Shepard B. Clough, "Retardative Factors in French Economic Development in the Nineteenth and Twentieth Centuries," *Journal of Economic History*, VI (1946), and David S. Landes, "French Entrepreneurship and Industrial Growth in the Nineteenth Century," *Journal of Economic History*, IX (1949).

French social history is in the process of becoming refined, but most of the works on the subject are of an introductory nature. Among the more important are Charles Morazé, *La France Bourgeoise* (Paris, 1946), David S. Landes, "French Business and the Businessman: a Social and Cultural Analysis," and John B. Christopher, "The Dessication of the Bourgeois Spirit," in E. M. Earle, ed., *Modern France*, and Jesse R. Pitts, "Continuity and Change in Bourgeois France," in Stanley Hoffman *et al.*, *In Search of France*, all of which provide insight into the conservative nature of the bourgeoisie. Gordon Wright, *Rural Revolution in France; the French Peasant in the Twentieth Century* (Stanford, 1964), contains a valuable introductory chapter on the condition of the peasants at the turn of the century. Edouard Dolléans, *Histoire du travail en France* (Paris, 1953–55), 2 volumes, and Val T. Lorwin, *The French Labor Movement* (Cambridge, Mass., 1954), are useful studies of the condition of the working class and the development of the trade union movement.

More studies are needed of French imperial expansion and French colonial policy at the turn of the century. Stephan H. Roberts, *A History of French Colonial Policy* (London, 1926), 2 volumes, is dated but still provides useful information about administrative policy. Henri Brunschwig, *French Colonialism, 1871–1914* (New York, 1966), is an interesting essay on the subject, but lacking in detail. Pierre Renouvin, *De 1871 à 1914:*

L'Apogée de l'Europe, volume VI (part 2) of P. Renouvin, ed., *Histoire des relations internationales* (Paris, 1955), is the best general account of European diplomatic history leading up to World War I. Other important studies are William L. Langer, *The Franco-Russian Alliance, 1890–1894* (Cambridge, Mass., 1929), and E. M. Carroll, *French Public Opinion and Foreign Affairs, 1870–1914* (New York, 1931). Dwight E. Lee, ed., *The Outbreak of the First World War* (Boston, 1958), includes selections from various conflicting accounts of the origins of World War I.

There is a growing body of literature on the subject of French political and social thought. Among the best works on the subject are Michael Curtis, *Three Against the Third Republic* (Princeton, 1959), a study of the anti-republican views of Barrès, Maurras, and Sorel; H. Stuart Hughes, *Consciousness and Society* (New York, 1957), a study of the effect of the revolt against positivism and the discovery of the subconscious on social thought at the turn of the century; Richard Humphrey, *George Sorel: A Prophet without Honor* (Cambridge, Mass., 1951); Hans Schmidt, *Péguy* (New Orleans, 1967); and Albert Thibaudet, *Les Idées politiques en France* (Paris, 1930). Among works relating to the intellectual and cultural history of France between 1870 and 1914 are Georges Duby and Robert Mandrou, *The History of French Civilization* (New York, 1962), and Ernst Robert Curtius, *The Civilization of France* (New York, 1962), both valuable surveys. Roger Shattuck, *The Banquet Years* (New York, 1961), is a beautifully written and extremely lucid account of the avant-garde movement. Other useful works include Henri Peyre, *The Contemporary French Novel* (New York, 1955), and François Mathey, *The Impressionists* (New York, 1961).

By far the best biography relating to the period between 1870 and 1914 is Harvey Goldberg, *The Life of Jaurès* (Madison, Wis., 1962) which not only examines the life of the Socialist leader, but also analyzes the politics of the Left from 1893 to 1914. Pierre Miquel, *Poincaré* (Paris, 1961), is another important work on the life and times of another important political leader, as is Henri Malo, *Thiers* (Paris, 1930). Other biographies are

Keith Eubank, *Paul Cambon* (Norman, Okla., 1962); Geoffrey Bruun, *Clemenceau* (Cambridge, Mass., 1943); C. W. Porter, *The Career of Théophile Delcassé* (Philadelphia, 1936); and Alain Silvera, *Daniel Halévy, A Gentleman-Commoner of the Third Republic* (Ithaca, N. Y., 1967).

There are many novels which are of importance to the historian of the period. Mention must be made of Maurice Barrès, *Le Roman de l'energie nationale;* Paul Bourget, *Le Disciple;* the many novels of Anatole France; Roger Martin du Gard, *Jean Barois* and *Les Thibault;* and Marcel Proust, *Remembrance of Things Past.*

Index

Action Française, 75–77, 85, 89, 127, 128, 133
Ader, Clément, 115
Africa, 90, 93–95, 97, 98, 99, 105, 106, 108, 110
agriculture, 22–25, 28, 31, 32, 98
Alain, 124
Albert, Marcellin, 24
Alexander III, 103
Algeciras Conference, 93, 108
Algeria, 91, 92, 93, 98, 112
Alsace, 27, 62, 63, 64
Alsace-Lorraine, 1, 3, 20, 26, 48, 101, 104, 110
Amiens, Charter of, 36
anarchism, 52–53
André (General), 74
Annam, 95, 96
anticlericalism, 40–44, 55, 70–75, 85, 131
anti-semitism, 26, 62, 65, 67, 71, 76, 84, 126
Apollinaire, Guillaume, 122, 123, 127
Arabs, 91
aristocracy, 19, 29–31, 37
Army, French, 30, 71
  in Algeria, 91
  André and, 74
  Boulanger and, 48–49
  Dreyfus affair and, 62–67, 71
  Gallifet and, 71

Army, French *(cont.)*
  Grévy's appointments in, 44
  and Morocco, 93
  and Siege of Paris, 1–2
  Three-Year Law, 86
Asia, 45, 84, 97, 98, 99, 105–110
Assembly, National
  Bismarck's armistice terms and, 2–5
  and election of President, 15–18
  and Dreyfus affair, 66
  and the Méline Tariff, 25
  and Monarchist majority, 11–12
  and pension for Pasteur, 114
  Republican majority in, 39
  and resignation of Thiers, 10–11
  urbanization and, 8
Assumptionists, 54, 71
Aulard, Alphonse, 117–118
Austria-Hungary, 20, 99, 102, 103, 109, 110, 111
automobiles, 28, 115

Balkans, 85, 86, 88, 103, 109, 110, 111
banking, 26
Bardo, Treaty of, 92
Barrès, Maurice, 67, 68, 122, 126–127, 133
Barthou, Louis, 56, 68
Bazaine (Marshal), 1, 2
Belgium, 27, 94, 105

141

belle époque, la, 28, 129, 130
Benda, Jules, 128
Bergson, Henri, 121
Berlin, Conference, 94
Berthelot, Marcelin, 113–114
bicycle, 114, 115
Bismarck, Otto von, 1, 2, 3, 27, 48, 51, 99–103
Blanqui Auguste, 57
Blériot, Louis, 115
Boer Republics, 113
Boisdeffre (General), 64, 66, 102, 103
Bonaparte, Jerome, 46, 49
Bonaparte, Mathilde, 128
Bonapartism, 12, 52, 132
Bonapartists, 30, 54, 132–133
    and Catholicism, 41
    and the Dreyfus affair, 68
    and the *Droite constitutionelle,* 54
    economic interests of, 31, 33, 37
    and elections, 4, 11–13, 16
    and *union des droites,* 46
Bordeaux, 3, 4
Boulanger (General), 47–51
Boulangism, 45, 47–52, 90, 101, 102, 126, 132
bourgeoise values, 34
bourgeoisie, 19, 21, 33–34, 37, 77, 131
Bourget, Paul, 68, 122
Bourses du Travail, 35
Brazza-Savorgnan, Pierre de, 94
Briand, Aristide, 80, 83, 84
Broglie, Albert de, 11, 13, 31, 87
Brunetière, Ferdinand, 68
Buisson, Ferdinand, 78

Caillaux, Joseph, 70, 87, 88, 108, 109
Calmette, Gaston, 88
Cambodia, 96
Catholicism, 30, 41, 42, 43, 72, 74, 75, 77
Catholics, 26, 41, 47, 53, 54, 60, 68, 71, 72, 74, 75

Cavaignac, Godefroy, 65, 66
Chamber of Deputies, 13–17, 83, 87, 98, 126, 134
    Algerian representation in, 91
    anticlerical sentiments of, 13
    bombing of, 55
    Boulangist attack on, 50
    and Combes ministry, 72–74
    elections of 1876, 13
    elections of 1881, 39
    elections of 1885, 46, 55, 58
    elections of 1889, 52
    elections of 1893, 58–59
    elections of 1914, 88
    and funds for Institut Pasteur, 116
    and income tax, 16
    Investigation of Panama Company, 61
    and laical legislation, 42–43, 72–73
    method of election, 16–17
    and *scrutin d'arondissment,* 72
    and *seize mai* crisis, 13–14, 16
    Socialist defense of strikes in, 81
    and Three-Year Law, 86
    and Waldeck-Rousseau ministry, 70
Chambord, Comte de, 10, 30, 41, 46
    and the white flag incident, 11
Charles X, 10, 30, 90
Chartier, Émile-Auguste, 124
China, 45, 95, 96, 97
Christian democracy, 60, 67, 75
Church, Catholic, 32, 40–43, 53, 71–75, 89
    and *Action Française,* 77, 84
    and aristocracy, 30
    and education, 13, 41–42, 71–73
    missionary efforts of, 84
    political influence of, 43
    and the *Ralliement,* 56, 68, 71
    against revisionism, 68
    role of, in French life, 40–41
Claudel, Paul, 121

Clemenceau, Georges, 74, 78, 131
  and Boulanger, 47, 51
  defeat of, in 1893, 55
  and Panama scandal, 61–62
  as Premier, 82–84
  and publication of *J'accuse*, 65
  and rebellion in Midi, 24
  resignation from National Assembly, 3
  on unicameral legislature, 40
coal mining, 26–28
Cochin, Augustin, 117
Cochin, Denys, 88
Cochin-China, 95, 96, 97, 113
colonies, *see* Empire, French
Combes, Émile, 72, 73, 74, 77, 78
Comte, Auguste, 41, 67, 76, 116, 120
Concordat of 1801, 42, 43, 71, 73
Confédération Générale du Travail, 36–37, 60
Confédération Général des Vignérons du Midi, 24
Congo, 94, 109
Conservatives, 40, 44–49, 89, 126, 131–132
  and the *Action Française,* 76
  and Boulanger, 46–49, 52, 84
  and the *Droite constitutionelle,* 55
  effect of, on urbanization, 23
  and elections of 1877, 14
  and elections of 1881, 39
  and elections of 1885, 46
  and Ferry, 45
  and Gambetta, 44
  and laical legislation, 72, 74–75
  and nationalist revival, 85
  and the *Ralliement,* 52–56, 68
  and *union des droites,* 46
Constans, Ernest, 51
Constitutional Laws of 1875, 12, 15–17, 130
Courbet, Gustave, 118
Croix, La, 54, 68, 71, 76

Curie, Marie, 114, 115
Curie, Pierre, 114, 115

Daudet, Léon, 76
De Gaulle, Charles, 125
Delcassé, Théophile, 70, 106, 107
Délégation des gauches, 78–82
Demange (Maître), 62, 63, 66
Déroulède, Paul, 48, 51, 66, 76, 101, 104
Diégo-Suarez, 95
D'Indy, Vincent, 121
Dreyfus, Alfred, 62–67
Dreyfus affair, 30, 61–69, 70, 71, 77, 84, 89, 90, 99, 105, 124, 125, 132
  Colonel Henry and, 65–66, 76
  Colonel Picquart and, 63–65
  effect of press, 67–68
  effect on military service, 86
  the Esterhazy note and, 63–65
  intellectuals and, 68, 128
  second court-martial, 66
Dreyfusards, 85, 124, 132, 134
Droite constitutionnelle, 53–55
Drumont, Edouard, 67, 71
Durkheim, Émile, 119–120

École Normale Supérieure, 58, 114, 121, 124
Egypt, 92–93, 100, 101, 104, 105, 106
Eiffel Tower, 113
elections of 1881, 39
elections of 1885, 45, 46, 49, 55, 58
elections of 1889, 52
elections of 1893, 54, 55, 56, 61, 88
elections of 1898, 54, 56
elections of 1902, 72
elections of 1906, 75
elections of 1914, 86, 87, 88
Empire, French, 26, 90–99, 100, 110, 113
Empire, Second, 4, 15, 20, 32, 96, 112, 115
Enlightenment, 41, 88, 116

Entente Cordiale, 106, 107
ésprit nouveau, 56
Esterhazy (Commandant), 63, 64, 65
Europe,
  and balance of power, 90, 100–101
  and coal supply, 27
  and economic recession, 25
  and educational trend, 43
  and Industrial Revolution, 19, 130
  and land tenure system, 22
Exposition of 1878, 14, 112
Exposition of 1889, 112–113
Exposition of 1900, 113

Fallières, Armand, 85
Fashoda, 99, 105, 106
Faure, Félix, 64, 66
fauvisme, 123
Favre, Jules, 1, 2
Fédération des Associations Viticoles,
  24
Fédération électorale, 54, 56
Ferry, Jules, 42, 44–45, 64, 96, 98,
  101, 116
First Republic, *see* Republic, First
Flaubert, Gustave, 118
Foreign Ministry, 105
France, Anatole, 122, 128
Franco-Prussian War, 1–8, 26, 32,
  116, 118
Franco-Russian Alliance, 102–103,
  107, 110, 111
Frankfurt, Treaty of, 3, 27, 100
Freemasons, 67, 74
Freycinet, Charles de, 48

Gallifet (General), 70 ,71, 74
Gambetta, Leon, 55, 56, 58, 70, 120
  death of, 45
  and election of 1881, 40
  and establishment of Third Repub-
    lic, 12
  and Franco-Prussian War, 1–4, 115
  and laical laws, 43

Gambetta, Leon (*cont.*)
  political organization of, 11
  strong leadership of, 44–45
Germany, 27–28, 45, 116, 117
  and Dreyfus affair, 62–63
  economic condition, 25, 27–29, 34
  emergence of fascism in, 134
  and Franco-Prussian War, 3
  French relationship with, 48, 51,
    84–86, 100–110
  and imperialism, 87, 90, 92
  population of, 20–22
  represented in Exposition of 1900,
    113
  and urban development, 21, 34
Gibraltar, 93
Gide, André, 68, 122
Goncourt, Edmond de, 118
Government of National Defense, 1,
  2, 3
Great Britain, 34, 99, 116
  agriculture of, 23
  diplomatic relations with France,
    100–108
  economic development of, 27–29
  and imperialism, 90, 92–96
  population of, 20–22
  and urbanization, 21–22
  and World War I, 110
Grévy, Jules, 14, 39, 44, 46, 47
Guesde, Jules, 57–58, 59, 79, 80, 81,
  88
Guinea, 94

Hanoi, 96, 97
Hanotaux, Gabriel, 105
Henry (Colonel), 64, 65, 66, 76
Herz, Cornelius, 61, 62
Holstein, Friedrich von, 102
Hué, Treaty of, 96
Hugo, Victor, 118

Impressionism, 119
income tax debate, 86–89

India, 90
Indo-China, 84, 95–97, 98, 99, 101, 104
industrial development, 25–28, 34, 98
Industrial Revolution, 19, 34
Institut Pasteur, 114
interpellation, 17, 18
Iran, Shah of, 112, 113
iron, 27
Italy, 23, 24, 73, 92, 100, 106, 107, 134
Ivory Coast, 94

Jacobin, 3, 8, 9, 52, 84, 131, 132
Japan, 97, 107
Jarry, Alfred, 120, 127
Jaurès, Jean, 58–60, 121
    and anti-Dreyfusards, 69
    Clemenceau and, 82
    defense of Millerand, 79–80
    election to Chamber, 58
    and emphasis on economic and social problems, 118
    and French Socialism, 59–60
    opposition to war, 81, 86–87, 88
    and the *Ralliement*, 77
    and SFIO, 83
July Monarchy, 15

Khedive Ismail, 92, 93
Kitchener (General), 104, 105
Kronstadt, 103

laical legislation, 42–44, 45, 54, 71–73
Lammenais, Félicité de, 41
Lamy, Étienne, 54, 56
Lansdowne, Marquis of, 106
Laos, 96, 104
Lavigerie (Cardinal), 53, 54, 55
Lavisse, Ernest, 117
League of Patriots, 48, 51, 66, 76, 101
legitimists, 10, 11

Leo XIII, 53, 54, 60, 71, 72, 73
Leopold II, 94, 112
Leroy- Beaulieu, Paul, 21
Lesseps, Ferdinand de, 61, 92
Libre Parole, Le, 62, 67, 68, 71
Ligue pour la défense des droits de l'homme, 68
Ligue de la Patrie française, 68, 76
Lille, 21, 23
Lorraine, 27, 85, 126
Loti, Pierre, 122
Loubet, Émile, 66, 70, 73, 106
Louis XIV, 90, 95
Louis XVI, 95
Louis-Philippe, 2, 10, 30, 48, 92
luxury goods, 28
Lyautey, Louis Hubert, 99

MacMahon (Marshal), 11–14, 16, 31, 101
Madagascar, 95
Mallarmé, Stéphane, 122
Marchand (Commandant), 105
Maritain, Jacques, 122
Marx, Karl, 6, 7, 8, 40, 81
Marxism, 7–8, 33, 34, 57, 58, 79, 80, 125
Mathiez, Albert, 118
Maupassant, Guy de, 118
Maurras, Charles, 67, 76, 84, 120, 127
Mekong Delta, 95
Meliès, Georges, 115
Méline, Jules, 56, 64, 65, 68, 75, 77, 85
Méline tariff, 23, 25, 38, 56
Mercier (General), 63, 66
Merry del Val (Cardinal), 73
Meyer, Arthur, 50
Michelin, Edouard, 114
Millerand, Alexandre, 59, 70, 79, 80
ministerial responsibility, 13, 16, 17, 134

Ministry of Agriculture, 25
Ministry of Colonies, 95
Ministry of Interior, 91
Ministry of Labor, 80
Monarchists, 9–16, 41, 42, 133
    and the *Action Française*, 76
    and the Comte de Paris, 46, 49
    division of, 10–12
    and the Dreyfus affair, 68
    and the *Droite constitutionelle*, 53–54
    and elections of 1871, 3–5
    and elections of 1876, 13
    and the *seize mai* crisis, 12–14
Monod, Gabriel, 117
Morocco, 84, 85, 87, 93–94, 99, 106, 107, 108, 133
Mun, Albert de, 30, 60

Napoleon I, 22, 41, 49, 92, 134
Napoleon III, 4, 12, 15, 25, 112, 132, 134
National Guard, 5, 6, 7
nationalist revival, 84–86, 87
Nietzsche, Friedrich, 120
Nile River, 94, 104
North Africa, 45, 47, 92, 93, 97, 99, 104, 106, 107

Oeuvres des cercles, 60
Old Regime, 10, 22, 28, 29, 30, 34, 37, 61, 71, 116, 127, 134
Opportunists, 68, 77, 131
    definition of, 40
    and the *Droite constitutionelle,* 55
    Ferry and, 42, 45
    Jaurès and, 58
    and laical legislation, 43, 72
    Poincaré and, 85
    and the *Ralliement,* 54–56
Orléanism, 33

Orléanists, 87
    the Comte de Paris and, 10, 30, 41, 46
    and the constitutional laws, 12, 18, 130
    and the *Droite constitutionelle,* 54
    and economic interests, 31, 37
    Thiers, 4–5
Ottoman Empire, 91, 92, 109

painting, French, 118–119, 123
Panama Company, 61, 62
Panama scandal, 61–62
Panther, 108
Paris, 21, 91, 113, 114, 115, 116, 127, 128, 134
Paris Commune, 4–9, 35, 47, 57
Paris, Comte de, 11, 41, 46, 49
Paris, siege of, 1, 2, 3, 47
Pasteur, Louis, 114
peasantry, 19, 31–32, 37, 45, 49, 51, 60, 81, 82, 83, 131
Péguy, Charles, 68, 124, 125, 127
Perrin, Jean, 114
Picquart (Colonel), 63, 64, 65
Piou, Jacques, 33, 53, 54, 56, 62, 75
Pius X, 73, 74
Poincaré, Henri, 144
Poincaré, Raymond, 16, 56, 68, 70, 77, 85, 86, 88, 89, 109, 111
population growth, 20–22
positivism, 42, 112, 114, 115, 116, 119, 120, 121, 133
President of the Republic, 11–16, 40
Prince Imperial, 12, 46
Prince of Wales, 112
proletariat, 19, 34–37, 49, 51, 81, 82, 83
Proudhon, Pierre-Joseph, 6, 57
Proust, Marcel, 68, 123, 126
Prussian army, 1, 2, 4, 5, 7, 9, 44

Quai d'Orsay, 106, 107

Radicals, 74, 118, 131
  Boulanger and, 48–49
  Clemenceau and, 3, 47
  in disagreement with Socialists,
      78–82, 84, 86–89
  and elections of 1885, 55
  and elections of 1906, 82
  and elections of 1914, 88
  Ferry and, 45
  and Gallifet, 70
  Gambetta and, 44
  and income tax, 87
  and laical legislation, 43, 69, 72
  and nationalist revival, 86
  origin of, 40
  and social legislation, 78–80
railroads, 25–26, 27, 31
Ralliement, 52–56, 71, 77, 85
Red River, 95, 97
Reinach, Jacques de, 61, 62
Renan, Ernest, 116, 117, 122
Republic, First, 1, 5
Republic, Second, 8, 15
Republicanism, 11
Republicans, 12, 14, 39–41, 49, 59,
      101
  and anticlerical campaign, 78
  and the Catholic Church, 41
  and the *Droite constitutionelle,* 55
  and elections of 1876, 13
  and elections of 1877, 14
  and elections of 1881, 39
  and elections of 1885, 46
  and elections of 1889, 50, 52
  electoral college dominated by, 16
  and Gambetta, 40
  and nationalist revival, 85–87
  and the *Ralliement,* 54–56
  and revolutionary ideal, 130–131,
      133
  and Thiers' funeral, 14
  and urbanization, 23
Rerum novarum, 60

Restoration, 15
Revolution, French, 34, 68, 131, 133
  Catholic Church and, 56
  centenary of, 112
  constitutional monarchy during, 10
  and legislative body, 15
  Paris Commune and, 6
  Sans culottes of, 5
  studies of, 117–118
Revolution of 1830, 30
Rimbaud, Arthur, 122
Rochefort, Henri de, 47, 50
Rouvier, Maurice, 49, 74, 107
Russia, 20, 24, 98–104, 106–111, 113,
      131

Sacré-Coeur, Church of, 15
Sadi-Carnot (President), 45, 47, 53
Saigon, 97, 98
Saint-Mandé program, 59
Salon de l'Aeronautique, 115
Sangnier, Marc, 75
Sarajevo, 110
Scheurer-Kestner (Senator), 64
Schnaebelé, Guillaume, 48, 101
Schwartzkoppen (Colonel), 62, 63
scrutin d'arrondissement, 17, 18, 72
scrutin de liste, 17, 44, 45
Second Empire, *see* Empire, Second
Second Republic, *see* Republic, Sec-
      ond
*Section française de l'internationale
      ouvrière,* 81, 88
  formation of, 80
seize mai crisis, 12–15, 16, 101
Senate, 12, 13, 16, 29, 40, 72, 78, 86,
      91
Senegal, 94, 112
Septennate, Law of, 11, 12
Serbia, 109, 110
Siam, 96, 104
Simon, Jules, 13
Socialism, 57–60, 125

Socialists, 36–37, 55, 57–60, 70, 77–84, 86–89, 131, 132
  and anticlericalism, 72, 78, 125
  and anti-Dreyfusards, 69
  and elections of 1893, 58
  and elections of 1896, 59
  and elections of 1914, 88
  and formation of SFIO, 88
  impact of Marxism on, 57
  and "ministerialism," 79–80
  and nationalist revival, 86
  and rejection of violence, 37
  and social legislation, 58–60, 74, 87–88
  and strikes in Chamber of Deputies, 81
Somaliland, 95
Sorel, Georges, 68, 125–126, 127, 128
Spain, 23, 24, 93, 108, 134
Spuller, Eugène, 56, 75
steel, 27
Stravinsky, Igor, 127
Suez Canal, 92
Syllabus of Errors, 30, 117
symbolism, 122
syndicalism, 36, 37, 52, 59, 82, 89, 131, 133

Taine, Hippolyte, 116, 117, 120
Tangiers, 107
tariffs, 29, 98
textile industry, 27–28
Thiers, Adolphe, 2–12, 14, 33, 34, 40, 55, 100, 130
Three-Year Law, 86, 88, 110
Tientsin, Treaty of, 96
Tocqueville, Alexis de, 134

Tonkin, 95, 96, 97, 99
trade union movement, 35–37, 133
  and collective bargaining, 82–83
  legislation, 35, 55
  setback after Paris Commune, 35
  and strikes, 83, 125
  suspicion of bourgeois intellectuals, 59–60, 80
Triple Alliance, 99, 100, 102, 108, 109
Triple Entente, 108
Tunis, Bey of, 91, 92
Tunisia, 91, 92, 93, 94, 101

union des droites, 46
Union Générale, 26, 67
United States, 20, 24, 25, 28, 29, 34, 43, 116, 130
urban development, 8–9, 21
Uzès, Duchesse d', 50

Vatican, 1, 73, 74, 77
Verlaine, Paul, 122
Verne, Jules, 115
Versailles, 2, 3, 5, 95
Versailles government, 6, 7, 9
Vichy Regime, 134
Viviani, René, 80, 88, 110

Waldeck-Rousseau, René, 35, 66, 70, 71, 72, 77, 79, 87
West Indies, 90
Wilhelm II, 107, 113
Wilson, Daniel, 46, 47
World War I, 20, 34, 37, 72, 95, 99, 110

Zola, Émile, 35, 65, 118